Buy this book for the chapter on joy. It alon.
of the book. Keep it for how it inspires you to work toward the
beautiful vision of unity that Jesus desires for his messy but
glorious bride.

—Bethany Jenkins, vice president
of media, Veritas Forum

I deeply appreciate Dan Darling and wholeheartedly concur
with his call for greater love and grace among Bible-believing
Christians. Like many, I watched Dan go through his public
ordeal that in my opinion never should have happened in a
Christian ministry. Dan's experience brought back memories of
the criticism I received from many believers when thirty years
ago I did what I believed to be right in God's sight, through
intervention to save the lives of the unborn. "Friendly fire"
doesn't seem very friendly when it leaves casualties in its wake.
This book is about our need to love God and in the process learn
to love our fellow believers, including those we disagree with in
secondary areas. I highly recommend *Agents of Grace* as a tool
for fostering a more conciliatory spirit.

—Randy Alcorn, author, *Heaven*, *Happiness*,
If God Is Good, and *Deception*

Why would someone who has been wounded by Christians seek
to serve and unite our churches? The answer is the grace of
God. Dan Darling has written a helpful work calling us, from
Scripture, to see unity as a must-have, not a nice-to-have. He's
called us to love not just Christians but *those* Christians. You
know the ones. The ones who look different than you. The ones
who think differently than you. The ones who care about different issues than you. I remember once thinking about writing
a book called *Agents of Unity*. I'm delighted Dan has written it
for me, and he was right to champion God's grace as the banner.
May we all be agents of that grace so the world will know we
follow Jesus (John 13:35).

—Isaac Adams, pastor, Iron City Church (Birmingham, AL);
founder, United? We Pray (uwepray.org)

In such a contentious and divisive climate, it's refreshing to hear voices like Dan's calling the body of Christ to unity. *Agents of Grace* is a contemporary letter to the church, and it reminds us through Jesus that there is far more that unites us than divides us. Here, we're reminded how even when we disagree, Christ's love beckons his bride to biblical unity, virtues, and holiness as modeled in Scripture. Dan's book affirms that the spiritual battle is real, but our fight is not with each other; united in Christ, we stand against an enemy who seeks to divide us. *Agents of Grace* offers the church common ground, through common grace, to engage the common good for God's glory.

—Christina Crenshaw, PhD, cultural engagement
and leadership associate, Dallas Theological
Seminary's Hendricks Center

The season we find ourselves in demands agents of grace and ambassadors of peace if we are going to bridge the divides we face today. This isn't foreign to our faith but core to it. Peacemaking and bridge building are signs the kingdom has come. Why are they so foreign to us as everyday followers of Jesus? Dan gives us great hope and help doing these very things. Read it and, more important, practice it.

—Bob Roberts, global senior pastor, Northwood Church;
founder, Glocalnet/Multifaith Neighbors Network

In a time when tribalism, hyperpartisanism, and us-against-them posturing are at a fever pitch, God's people need renewed vision for Christ- and beatitude-worthy engagement. In times like today, when gospel virtues like love, peace, forgiveness, joy, and humility are scarce, leaning into those same virtues by the power of Christ might be our best opportunity for faithful, fruitful witness. And? We will be happier for it! As usual, Daniel has provided an excellent resource for God's people for such a time as this.

—Scott Sauls, senior pastor, Christ Presbyterian
Church; author, *Jesus Outside the Lines* and
Beautiful People Don't Just Happen

Dan Darling writes with authenticity and about how we, as Christians with many differences and life experiences, can stay unified in Christ. At a time when politics and ideology often divide friends and families, Dan demonstrates Christians can hold strong to the words and life of Jesus as we navigate this modern culture. *Agents of Grace* will help you think critically, biblically, and gracefully at the same time, offering a renewed perspective of each and every image bearer we come into contact with each day.

—Ericka Andersen, author, *Reason to Return: Why Women Need the Church and the Church Needs Women*

I heard someone say a lot of people are willing to kill for Christ but very few are willing to die for Christ. So many of us perform on social media now, and there is an incentive for bravado and boorish behavior, getting attention for ourselves, not really for Christ and his church. Like the early Christians in their pagan world, we could shine a light in our pagan world and stand out by showing more grace. Grace seems to be a forgotten concept for a lot of Christians, and Dan Darling does an excellent job reminding us of its necessity and what it actually is.

—Erick Erickson, host, *The Erick Erickson Show*

Agents of Grace is a stirring call for Christians to manifest God's redemptive grace in the church and in society. Recognizing that genuine Christian unity must be coupled with doctrinal integrity, Daniel Darling offers thoughtful guidance for choosing the right theological fights and the manner in which to address the cultural issues of our day. Moreover, he appeals to followers of Christ to prioritize the virtues of love, peace, and forgiveness, together with lament, humility, and hope. Let us pray that readers will hear afresh and put into practice the Pauline exhortation "to make every effort to keep the unity of the Spirit through the bond of peace."

—David S. Dockery, president, International Alliance for Christian Education; Distinguished Professor of Theology, Southwestern Baptist Theological Seminary

Agents of Grace

How to Bridge Divides and Love as Jesus Loved

Daniel Darling

ZONDERVAN
BOOKS

ZONDERVAN BOOKS

Agents of Grace
Copyright © 2023 by Daniel Darling

Requests for information should be addressed to:
Zondervan, 3900 Sparks Dr. SE, Grand Rapids, Michigan 49546

Zondervan titles may be purchased in bulk for educational, business, fundraising, or sales promotional use. For information, please email SpecialMarkets@Zondervan.com.

ISBN 978-0-310-36632-4 (softcover)
ISBN 978-0-310-36634-8 (audio)
ISBN 978-0-310-36633-1 (ebook)

Published in association with the literary agency of Wolgemuth & Associates, Inc.

Cover design: Faceout Studio, Spencer Fuller
Interior design: Denise Froehlich

Printed in the United States of America

23 24 25 26 27 LBC 5 4 3 2 1

To my amazing wife,
Angela,
an agent of grace

Contents

Foreword by J. D. Greear

In many ways, the evangelical church is more divided than ever. The last several years—2020 especially—have revealed a lot of fractures and fissures. Truth be told, many of these divisions already existed, but factors like COVID-19 and racial violence brought them to the surface. A recent (post-COVID) LifeWay study among pastors shows that church unity is their number 1 concern, even more than other issues such as money or growth or secularization.[1]

Like many pastors, I went into the COVID-19 pandemic in early 2020 with such high hopes for spiritual renewal. We were going to reinvent church. Our members would really be able to slow down and focus on their relationship with the Lord. Christians would learn to self-feed and start multiplying house churches. Would it be tough? Sure. But it would also be awesome.

Well, as you are likely aware, that didn't happen. I'm encouraged by what God did in the church around the world during that season, but the disunity that was revealed in the American church was disturbing. Deep fissures surfaced—political and cultural. People who had worshiped together for years decided they couldn't anymore, and many "left loud." It made many of us ask, Can we really do this together? And if so, how? In 1 Corinthians 1:10, Paul tells us to "be united with the same understanding and the same conviction" (CSB). What does that mean in today's world?

It is interesting to me that these words are singular. Paul is not saying that we'll be unified by having the same understandings and same convictions on everything. Paul is saying, "Be of the same understanding and same conviction," singular. Why? Because it's about the gospel. Paul is telling the church to have the same understanding about the importance of the gospel over secondary things, and the same conviction about the primacy of the gospel.

In the pages that follow, my friend Dan Darling offers crucial insight on what it means to love our brothers and sisters in the Lord and to honor our Savior's desire that we proclaim his lordship by our unity. Dr. Darling, in his life and public witness, embodies the message of this book. He shows us that:

- *Unity* is not *uniformity, where everybody in the church agrees on everything.* That's not the biblical vision of the church. The New Testament church is a community where Jesus is so large that it makes disagreement on secondary things less important.

Jesus famously brought into his circle two disciples (Simon the Zealot and Matthew the tax collector) from opposite political sides. I told our church that what was most disappointing for me in 2020 was how so many church people were willing to walk away from their church over a relatively small disagreement, at least small in light of the gospel and eternity. We Christians say we hate "cancel culture," but it was amazing to me how so many of us canceled our church over disagreements about relatively small things, at least small in light of the gospel.

- *Unity* is not *relativism*. Relativism is when you say that everyone is right about everything. Frankly, that's ridiculous. There *are* right and wrong approaches to many things. The challenge is in the importance we give these things. Do we have the same conviction about the gospel? Unity is not relativism, it's understanding that the gospel is more important than all else.

- *Unity* is not *compromising the core tenets of the faith*. Some Christians think the only way we can be unified is by refusing to take clear stands on anything. But throughout his letter to the Corinthians, Paul identified a number of beliefs and said, "We have to agree on these or we've lost our identity as a witness to God's kingdom." In this book, Daniel Darling articulates those things that he calls "worthy fights" and those other issues about which Christians might have disagreements, but that are not worth fighting for. Christians need this book in these increasingly polarized times.

- *Unity* is not *sentimentality*. If you know Dan and have read his work, you know he's not afraid to speak up with courage about what is right and what is wrong. So *Agents of Grace* doesn't suggest that we paper over divisions, never talk about them, and just smile for the camera. Instead this book will help you understand what it means to love like Jesus calls us to love and to learn how to disagree well, especially in areas where Christians have disagreed for all of church history.
- *Unity* is *having the same conviction about the gospel*, the same understanding about its importance, and then attempting to think about everything else in line with that.

I was eager to endorse *Agents of Grace* because I think we're at a defining moment in the evangelical movement. Who are we? What are we going to be about? Can we obey Jesus' command to demonstrate the gospel by our love for each other?

In John 17, Jesus, right before the nails were put into his hands and feet, asked God to unify his church. He wasn't having a sentimental, kum-ba-yah experience or nostalgic yearning. He was asking God to unify us so that the world would know the truth about him. A unified church, he said, would display his power to the nations. A unified church is not a convenience or lofty aspiration, it's a matter of world salvation.

Jesus' unity, of course, was not to be a unity at all costs. Truth, he said, must be the center of unity (John 17:17). But gospel maturity means knowing which things should divide us and which should not.

Christian believer, we have been given a message about God—the God who spoke the world into existence—a message about how he loved humanity, you and me, so much that he gave his one and only Son to redeem us from our sins. It's a message about the only God and the only way of salvation. That message unites us not because other messages aren't important but because that one is primary. In the span of eternity, it's the only one that matters. And we, the church, are the only ones with that message.

So if we are going to divide, let it be over something worthy of division. If we're going to be at war, let us be at war against the principalities and powers that impede gospel proclamation. If we're going to take up arms, then let's take up arms against the evil one by taking up our Bibles, in the power of the Holy Spirit, to advance God's kingdom. Let's take the battle against sin, against Satan, and against self-serving shibboleths as we march in pursuit of the great commission of our king, Jesus.

Jesus prayed for the unity of the church, and I want to pursue it for his glory. There are truths we must never compromise, but for the sake of people hearing about Jesus, I am ready to downplay certain preferences and properly categorize secondary convictions so that I can stand united with all on the essential message about Jesus.

Join me in heeding Daniel Darling's admonition to be an agent of grace and to embody those words attributed to the early church: "In essentials, unity; in nonessentials, liberty; in all things, charity."

Preface

Cracked by Grace

> *Man is born broken. He lives by mending.*
> *The grace of God is glue!*
>
> —**Eugene O'Neill,** *The Great God Brown*

I've wanted to write this book for a long time but put it off for various reasons until unforeseen events finally propelled me: I was let go, in a very public way, from a position at a Christian ministry. It was a painful time, one that I wish hadn't splashed across the pages of leading newspapers and websites and dominated social media for a few weeks. When, so many years ago, I walked down a dusty aisle at summer camp to commit my life to ministry, I didn't dream that my calling to follow Jesus would include being a breaking story in the *New York Times*. But there it was.

This experience and the last few years of rough-and-tumble conflicts among Christians have me thinking about Jesus' command to love one another. This book is not a juicy tell-all. It's not a revenge memoir. It's a plea from one Christian to another that we take seriously the words of Scripture that urge us to cling to what unites us as God's people rather than focus on what divides us.

In my office is a photo frame, given to me by my wife last Father's Day. It contains the lyrics to the hymn "Amazing Grace," written by the former slave trader John Newton. This is the heart of our faith: amazing grace, how sweet the sound, that saved a wretch like me. The frame is cracked at one end, a casualty of a cross-country move from Tennessee to Texas, where I started a new job as director of the Land Center for Cultural Engagement at Southwestern Seminary. And yet cracked grace is an apt metaphor for Christians, isn't it? We bear the message of good news, but we, the messengers, the vessels that bear this message, are, well, a bit cracked. "Fragile clay jars" (2 Cor. 4:7 NLT) is the way the apostle Paul describes us.

You'll need to know, up front, that I'm hopelessly in love with the church. And when I say the church, I'm talking not only about the worldwide communion of saints in heaven and on earth, made up of every nation, tribe, and tongue, but also about the local church. The addresses and buildings have changed for me over the years, from Illinois to Tennessee to Texas to whatever church I happen to be visiting to speak. I've been walking up the aisles, sitting in cramped pews, belting out verses of hymns since the moment I could form words. Despite the church's visible cracks, the sins and failures within her walls, and even with four and a half decades of church already in me, I still can't wait for Sunday.

I think it's appropriate, before we talk about what it means to love as Jesus loved, before we talk about living as agents of grace in a fractured world, before we challenge ourselves to pursue unity among followers of Christ, that you get to know me a little bit. My story is one of God's sovereignty and grace. When I reflect on my life, I can't help but see the finger of God writing my life's story before I was born. That story begins in 1971 in Chicago, before I was born. My father, abandoned by his alcoholic father and raised by an equally troubled stepfather, only ever knew dysfunction. At fourteen he got himself up early to work at a bakery, giving his mother every penny so she could supplement her earnings as a crossing guard and whatever her new husband, a mailman, would hand over after his gambling at the race track.

But in the midst of this mess, a message of hope arrived, delivered by a captivating, fiery, silver-tongued preacher named Billy Graham. He shared a simple gospel for a world troubled by Vietnam, race riots, and Watergate. Graham's message was sweeping the globe, and it swept right into a family on a trajectory toward failure. In 1971, at the Billy Graham Crusade at the McCormick Center in Chicago, Dad walked forward with his mother. He found Jesus. Or rather, Jesus found him.

A few years ago, when Graham died, I looked up on YouTube the sermon Graham gave the night my dad went forward. I sat there watching it on my phone, tears streaming down my face as I imagined my father, almost a half century earlier, hearing that good news and finding salvation in Christ. On my office wall is a framed black-and-white image of the crowd from that night, a gift from a friend at the Billy Graham Evangelistic Association. Somewhere out there, among that throng of people, is my father.

Dad, in those early days, was a Jesus freak, so intoxicated by his newfound faith. He met my mother, a Jewish girl also swept up in the Jesus movement, and they got married. Her grandparents, my great-grandparents, had emigrated to America at the turn of the twentieth century, escaping the pogroms in Poland and Russia. My grandfather, a tank commander in World War II, was a charter member of what we now call the Greatest Generation, enduring the Great Depression and serving his country when summoned to war against fascism. He and my grandmother raised their children on Chicago's North Shore.

Mom and Dad were not exactly what you would call a match: an outspoken new convert and a shy Jewish girl. If dating apps existed in the early 1970s, both would have swiped right and I wouldn't exist. But my mother was charmed by Dad's earthy authenticity and found her spiritual questions answered by the same fresh gospel Dad wore on his sleeve in those days. Her conversion to Christianity was a mini scandal, as was her marriage to my father. But over time, Dad's steady faithfulness won over my grandparents, who professed faith in Christ before they passed away in the early 2000s.

My parents joined the first church they ever found, a fledgling independent Baptist church in the northwest suburbs of Chicago led by a charismatic young pastor from Kentucky. With the zeal of first-generation converts, they imbibed everything they heard. They were pretty strict. We had no TV in our home, listened only to certain kinds of Christian music, and never visited a movie theater. I had to hide my Amy Grant CDs.

So this is where you'd expect me to say that I escaped all of this, deconstructing the ridiculous beliefs of my youth. But that is not my story. I still love those old pews, the hymns that speak of God's matchless grace, the gospel word that reminds me of God's love on my worst days. I may not be as strict as my parents were in those early days—Southern Baptists wear jeans, listen to good music, and some of us even dance—but I'm thankful for the things I learned as a child that stuck: the habit of attending church every week, seeing my father open his Bible every morning, and the way the gospel fills the cracks in my soul with grace. Billy Graham brought my parents to Jesus, and my parents brought me to Jesus. I'm thankful for God's steady hand guiding me along on a journey I couldn't have planned myself.

Today I'm a father, trying my best, with my wife, to point our children to the same gospel that changed Dad's life so many decades ago and is still changing mine. I'm a pastor, an author, and a professor. But most important, I'm a member of this wonderful yet messy family that stretches around the globe and into the great chorus in heaven, the worldwide body of Christ.

I've seen up close the good, the bad, and the ugly of our

movement. I've endured backstage divas. I've been fired unjustly. I've been attacked by Christians online. Still, the people of God are my people, and the church is my home, Sunday after Sunday, year after year. The church is the place where I often stumble in, weary, squeezed by the pressures of life, uncertain of the future, and it is where I keep hearing God speak to me from his Word, where timeless lyrics keep healing my heart, and where the beauty of Christian orthodoxy keeps anchoring my soul.

The last few years have seen so much conflict among believers, and the cultural fault lines run through families and churches and communities. Perhaps you have fresh pain from a wound inflicted by a brother or sister in Christ. Perhaps you are increasingly cynical about the scandals, the controversies, and the tribalism of many Christians. Or maybe you know that you are supposed to love your fellow believers, but you wonder how it's possible to love *those* particular Christians who annoy you so much. Perhaps you are tired of the fighting and hope to be a bridge builder among the people of God. Perhaps, like me, you wonder how we can live out the lyrics of that hymn, how we can be agents of grace when we are, like the frame in my office, so cracked.

I'm writing to say that God is still at work in the world and to say that Christian love and spiritual unity are still worth pursuing. While I've been hurt by Christians, I've also been immensely blessed by Christians. Brothers and sisters in Christ have been there for me in my pain: single mothers who made meals when my wife endured a serious illness; small-group leaders who gave me money when I was suddenly unemployed and scared; a pastor who called and preached the Word of God to me when I was in despair. I've been blessed by wise matriarchs with arthritic knees who called down spiritual fire from heaven on my behalf when I was weak. I've been healed by friends who left everything and came to my side when I needed hope.

Sure, there have been some who, in moments of my despair, sounded like the negative cast who surrounded Job, but so many more have been like the friends of David, supporting, encouraging, and strengthening me in moments of deepest need. Perhaps this is your experience as well.

It is Christians who taught me to serve and sacrifice, and it is in church where I first learned that because of Jesus' resurrection, all that is broken will be made new again. It is in church that I first understood that the most vulnerable among us—babies and refugees and orphans—have full dignity from their creator. It is in church that I have been reminded, over and over, that I am part of a forever family, this wild and messy gathering of flawed humans from every nation, tribe, and tongue throughout history.

If we are not careful, if our perception of the church is formed only by bad headlines, we will let the darkness overshadow the slivers of light, the pinpricks of hope. We will overlook the way the Spirit of God is moving in the world through ordinary people.

We shouldn't paper over scandals and corruption as

though they didn't happen. Paul didn't spare the church at Corinth. The book of Revelation didn't spare those seven churches. I weep over the stories of people wounded by those who claim the name of Christ, by the sheep spiritually devoured by wolves. I see why, for too many, the church has been a place of pain.

Yet the same Spirit who has awakened every generation since Pentecost, who has breathed gospel fire through sinners around the globe, is doing his work in this age. Jesus declared that the church is unlike other movements or organizations, which fade and fall through history. "I will build my church," the man from Nazareth says, "and the gates of hell shall not prevail against it" (Matt. 16:18 KJV).

Perhaps this is why the tears flow when I hear the lyrics that beckon me back to the cross: "I hear the Savior say, 'Thy strength indeed is small, child of weakness, watch and pray, find in me thine all in all.'" I remain in the church not because I refuse to see its many obvious flaws. I am here simply because I have nowhere else to go. I still believe Jesus Christ walked out of that borrowed tomb and is at work transforming the hearts of sinful people.

This one who rose from the grave still anguishes in love over his bride, including all those people we find too annoying to love. Jesus calls them my brothers and my sisters, and so must I. For better or for worse, these are my people.

Consider this book a family letter to remind us what we are called to be. We live in an age of disunity, with perverse incentives to turn on each other. But the Bible calls us to love each other in such a way as to arouse the attention of those who do not follow Jesus. Unity in the body of Christ is not just a nice thing if we get to it. Unity is a command, a way of life, a practice.

I've divided this book into two sections—one about worthy virtues and one about worthy fights—to reflect the tension of living as a faithful Christian. We are called both to love with an otherworldly love and to courageously fight for truth. What does love require? What does unity look like? How can we get along with believers with whom we disagree? Which conflicts with fellow Christians are worth engaging and which are frivolous? How do we process the pain inflicted on us by other believers? These are all questions I hope to address from Scripture.

My prayer is for God's Spirit to blow a fresh wind across our divides, that as we weep over the ways Christians bite and devour (Gal. 5:15), we might commit ourselves to Jesus' call to love one another.

Part 1

Worthy Virtues

Chapter 1

What Does Love Require?

Virtue: Love

> *The one who loves God must also love his brother and sister.*
>
> **—1 John 4:21 NASB**

> *Love—and the unity it attests to—is the mark Christ gave Christians to wear before the world. Only with this mark may the world know that Christians are indeed Christians and Jesus was sent by the Father.*
>
> **—Francis Schaeffer,** *A Christian View of the Church*

Hey, man, I'm so sorry about our last conversation. I was wrong. Will you forgive me?"

This is a text I just sent to a friend. Our friendship has been severely tested over the last few years. My guess is that you too are feeling this tension in your relationships. Otherwise you probably wouldn't have picked up this book.

American society, or perhaps we should broaden this to Western society, is increasingly riven by so many forces: social media, economic changes, secularism, populism, and a thousand other *isms*. We are having to ask ourselves what it looks like to live faithfully in an increasingly hostile world and how to navigate these tensions in our families, churches, and organizations. I've spent much of my life and career addressing the first question. For conversations about this, you might read my two books: *A Way with Words* and *The Dignity Revolution*.

It's the second question—how to handle division among God's people—that has led me to write this book. I'm heartbroken by the way Jesus' followers—who are called to be salt and light in a dark world—are caught up in the tribalism that afflicts the world.

When I think back on that conversation with my Christian brother, I feel regret, a sense of shame. This is someone I deeply love. We've gone through a lot together. Yet here I was so willing to rupture a friendship over a petty dispute. I was so dogmatic about something not worth being dogmatic about. This was a lack of love.

I was frustrated at his take on some current event, and he was equally frustrated with mine. So we quarreled. And the next day I regretted my words. Now that the dopamine hit of being right was long gone, the still voice of God tiptoed right up to my conscience and asked, *Was that necessary?*

This book has been burning within me. A sojourner in evangelical life for four and a half decades, having traveled a winding path among our many tribes, I'm deeply distressed by our family fights. The collateral damage is all around us. Too many lost friendships. Too many split churches. Too many discouraged pastors. Too many damaged church members. Too many young people walking away disillusioned by what they see.

You might be feeling this in your family, church, and community. Almost every week I hear from a father whose son won't speak to him because they disagree about social justice or politics, or a pastor whose church has beaten him up over a petty cultural preference, or a parachurch leader whose organization is split by warring factions. We all see this happening and yet it seems we like to blame our divisions on everyone else. It's the media companies. It's the other political party. It's that other evangelical tribe.

To be clear, quite a few social factors have brought us to this moment, but God's Word plainly points us to the real source: "What causes fights and quarrels among you?" the brother of Jesus asked the first-century church. "Don't they come from your desires that battle within you?" (James 4:1).

Yes, they do. James here is like a surgeon of the human heart, diagnosing our dilemma while knifing his way into places that make us uncomfortable. What's behind all our angst and unrest? It's the sin that, since Eden, has so marbled its way throughout the human experience. We fight because we are sinful. We are carnal. We choose the way of the serpent instead of the way of the Creator.

Before you misunderstand, the fights I'm talking about among Christians, the ones James is referring to here, are not what I like to call worthy fights, a topic we will explore in detail later. Conflict isn't always a sign of sin. Sometimes God's people must rise to defend "the faith that was once for all entrusted to God's holy people" (Jude 1:3). We shouldn't hesitate to "fight the good fight of the faith" (1 Tim. 6:12).

Yet if we are honest with ourselves, most battles among believers are not the good fights. As I write, I'm thinking of two Christian brothers I deeply admire, leaders whose work has shaped my life and theology. These two men agree on the essentials of the Christian faith. On a Venn diagram, their values nearly overlap. Yet they haven't spoken to each other in years. Former friends, they now see each other as foes, each too stubborn to do the work to rebuild their friendship. So they battle, in private conversations with peers and in subtle public jabs in social-media posts and columns. It's shameful and quite sad and, if I may be so bold, a terrible witness to a watching world: friends who once wrote books together and shared meals together going to war.

This is happening all over. It's happening in families, between parents and children. It's happening in churches, between rival factions. It's happening in Christian institutions. It's a daily occurrence online. And it's often skirmishes over nonessential matters, over styles and preferences and postures. Our public battles are often not about "the faith that was once for all entrusted to God's holy people" but about opinions delivered on Facebook.

We should tremble at the words of the apostle John, who was once known as an abrasive Son of Thunder. In one of his final letters to the church, this elder statesman urges the people of God to love, declaring that "the one who loves God *must* also love his brother and sister" (1 John 4:21 NASB, emphasis added). Must love:

- Even if your sister doesn't vote the way you do.
- Even if your brother annoys you with his opinions on Facebook.
- Even if your sister doesn't agree with your approach to worship.
- Even if your brother recommended a book you thought was terrible.

John's word reminds me of a favorite bluegrass hymn that asserts, "If you don't love your neighbor, you don't love God."[1]

The Bible says that we demonstrate our love for God by the way we love our fellow Christians. We should care about all human beings, because each is an image bearer of God (Gen. 1:26), but those who are our brothers and sisters in faith deserve our special affection (Gal. 6:10). According to Jesus, the way we love other Christians is supposed to be a witness to an unbelieving world (John 13:35). John is essentially saying to the church, "You are family. You are united by the blood of Jesus. You will live forever together in heaven."

John's words are sobering. I can talk all day about how much I love God, but if I don't love my Christian brothers and sisters, I'm not loving the God who redeemed them by his grace. I want to practice the words of 1 John.

This is why, in this season of my life, with all of my might and in the power of the Spirit, I'm more determined than ever to hang on to my relationships with other believers, despite the internal and external pressures to let them go. I hope you feel this way as well. This is what love requires.

A Friend Who Sticketh

Growing up, I memorized a lot of Scripture: in my Christian school, in Awana, in Sunday school, all of it from the King James Version. One of the phrases from the KJV that has stuck with me comes from Proverbs 18:24. "There is a friend that sticketh closer than a brother."

We don't say sticketh anymore, but the word stayed with me. In my mind, this old English word takes the concept of sticking and raises it a level or two. Sticketh makes me think of gum on the underside of a desk in fourth grade, or the stubborn price tag on a last-minute gift on Christmas Eve, or the kitchen table after my youngest daughter has finished off a plate of waffles.

Sticketh is the sound your sneakers make on the tile when you've stepped on spilled Coke. Sticketh is the dilemma you face when you've accidentally superglued your hands. Sticketh is your child after the cotton candy you reluctantly said yes to at the ballgame.

The root word in the original Hebrew, *dabeq*, implies a "holding fast" a "sticking to," to be "glued" or "cemented." It is used quite often in the Old Testament for things that cleave, such as Job's bones that cleaved to his skin (Job 19:20) or Psalm 119:25, where the psalmist says that his soul cleaves to the dust. It is an act of not letting go.[2]

If something sticketh, it ain't coming off. I don't like this term when it comes to syrup or snot or soft drinks, but it warms my heart when it makes me think of a friend so willing to be in my life that they ain't letting go. Do you know anyone like that?

I think of my wife, who slips meals into our room when I get COVID or who endures my crankiness when I'm on a book deadline. (Like right now.)

I think of my text-thread buddies, friends spread throughout the country. We call ourselves the GOAT group (GOAT meaning "greatest of all time"). We've all seen each other through hardship and loss and pain these last few years.

The writer of Proverbs is daydreaming about such a friend. The Scriptures are full of such relationships. There is Ruth, once a pagan from Moab, who says to her grieving and impoverished mother-in-law, fleeing back to her ancestral homeland, "Where you go I will go. . . . Your people will be my people" (Ruth 1:16–17). In other words, "Naomi, you can't get rid of me. I want what you want and I'll have what you have and no amount of disruption will keep me from being by your side." This is a friendship that sticketh. Ruth clung to Naomi because Naomi clung to God. Today we might say that Ruth was Naomi's "ride or die."

There is Jonathan, the would-be prince who resisted the jealous rage of his father, Saul, to stand by David. This friendship came at great cost to the heir apparent. He could have scratched and clawed for the throne. Jonathan could have enlisted in his father's futile war on God's next anointed king. Jonathan could have had David killed. Instead, he protected David with his own life. Jonathan saw God's hand of blessing on David and committed himself to staying with his friend. The politics of the moment couldn't, wouldn't break this friendship. Jonathan wasn't embarrassed by David.

We could also find an example in the relationship of Jesus with his disciples. Simon Peter said to Jesus, after many people fell away because of his hard teachings, "Lord, to whom shall we go? You have the words of eternal life" (John 6:68). Peter's words were tested when he denied Jesus in a moment of panic and terror, yet Jesus, the ultimate friend who sticks closer than a brother, restored Peter to fellowship when he appeared to him on the beach after his resurrection.

Like Peter's, all of our "sticking" friendships will face the limits of our frailties. We can't know how to love in this way without knowing the one who will never let us go:

> My command is this: Love each other as I have loved you. Greater love has no one than this: to lay down one's life for one's friends. You are my friends if you do what I command. I no longer call you servants, because a servant does not know his master's business. Instead, I have called you friends, for everything that I learned from my Father I have made known to you. You did not choose me, but I chose you and appointed you so that you might go and bear fruit—fruit that will last—and so that whatever you ask in my name the Father will give you. This is my command: Love each other.
>
> **—John 15:12–17**

"Love each other, as I have loved you." Jesus loves us with a sacrificial, everlasting, superhuman love. And he is empowering us to love each other this same way. In their book, *Why Does Friendship Matter?* Chris Firestone and Alex Pierce write, "Our vertical friendship with God organizes our horizontal friendships with others."[3]

I like that. When we love well—through thick and thin, ups and downs, pain and peril—we show the world an otherworldly kind of love. Love that sticketh like a brother is a signpost of another world. Conversely, our inability to love other Christians is a turn-off to those seeking God and might be a flashing red light of the state of our souls. Perhaps our inability to love could mean we've grown cold in our love for God.

As Far as It Depends on You

Recently, I participated in a reconciliation meeting, brokered by some other Christians, with someone with whom I'd had a disagreement. I felt then and still feel now that this man wronged me. I had some family and friends ask me, "Why are you doing this?" Honestly, I really didn't want to go to this meeting. I knew that facing this brother would dredge up hard things I wanted to forget. To be honest with you, I went, but my feet were dragging.

And yet I'm glad I did it. We talked through our differences. We shook hands and hugged. Does this mean everything is forgotten and we'll go on a camping trip together? Probably not. But I walked away from that meeting at peace. I can say that I harbor no ill will toward this brother.

What does love require? At the very least, love takes seriously Paul's words in Romans 12:18: "If it is possible, as far as it depends on you, live at peace with everyone." Love is often hard and painful work. It's way easier to let anger fester, to feed that resentment, to wrap my identity in my pain. My friend Scott Sauls says it like this: "Because Jesus Christ has loved us at our worst, we can love others at their worst. Because Jesus Christ has forgiven us for all of our wrongs, we can forgive others who have wronged us."[4]

I know what you are thinking right now, because I've thought it too. *This sounds naive. Not every relationship can be restored.* This is true. Some are so layered over with sin and its consequences that reconciliation is just not possible. Paul does say, in Romans 12:18, "as far as it depends on you." He had his own sharp disagreement with Barnabas, his mentor, the one who had shepherded him through his early Christian ministry (Acts 15). My sense is that Paul and Barnabas eventually did reunite, but we don't really know. And we have the hope that when Jesus returns, every broken friendship will be mended.

Love doesn't demand that we erase important boundaries. Sometimes we need to distance ourselves from toxic people. For instance, the New Testament instructs churches to withdraw fellowship from those engaging in ongoing moral sin (1 Cor. 5:11) and yet also urges the church to work to restore wayward brothers and sisters back to faith (Gal. 6:1).

Love sometimes requires us to communicate hard truths for the spiritual health of our brothers and sisters. Love sometimes requires confrontation. Love sometimes requires toughness for the sake of the flourishing of God's people.

But if we are honest with ourselves, if we are alone with our thoughts, we would have to admit that many, if not most, of the conflicts we are engaged in don't fit these narrow categories. A great majority of the online squabbles, the petty disputes that divide churches, and the gossip that fuels endless warfare among Christians are what is described in the Bible as "quarrelling about words" and "godless chatter" (2 Tim. 2:14, 16) and "foolish and stupid arguments" (v. 23).

Love also doesn't demand that every single Christian be our best friend. Jesus himself had various circles: the hundreds of followers, the twelve disciples, and then his inner circle of Peter, James, and John. There will be Christian people with whom and communities in which you feel most at home, and there will be Christian people with whom and communities in which you may not feel most at home. This is natural and normal if we remember that we are called to love both our friends close to us and other believers whom we may not necessarily consider our best friends.

The apostle Paul helps us think this through in his first letter to the Corinthian church, a polemic filled with rebuke for a sinful and wayward congregation. Amid chapters dealing with controversial topics such as spiritual gifts and the order of worship, he pauses with a chapter that seems somewhat out of place. This is the famous passage in Scripture quoted at weddings, the "love chapter." We sometimes miss Paul's larger point by forgetting the context. His letter is addressed specifically to Christians: "To the church of God in Corinth, to those sanctified in Christ Jesus and called to be his holy people, together with all those everywhere who call on the name of our Lord Jesus Christ—their Lord and ours" (1 Cor. 1:2).

These Christians, this church that Paul is addressing, were riven by divisions over the spiritual gifts and by tribalism and had yielded to the sensuality of the age. And in the midst of Paul's careful prescriptions on doctrine and worship, he pauses and urges them to be marked by love.

This is a passage we'd be wise to heed. The Bible is thoroughly unimpressed with spiritual giftedness or the size of our sacrifices or the scope of our generosity if we are not empowered by the love of Christ: "If I speak in the tongues of men or of angels, but do not have love, I am only a resounding gong or a clanging cymbal. If I have the gift of prophecy and can fathom all mysteries and all knowledge, and if I have a faith that can move mountains, but do not have love, I am nothing. If I give all I possess to the poor and give over my body to hardship that I may boast, but do not have love, I gain nothing" (1 Cor. 13:1–3).

It doesn't matter how tight our theology, it doesn't matter how active our activism, it doesn't matter how inspired our worship, if we are not motivated by love for our brothers and sisters, our work for the Lord is in vain. That is sobering to me. I don't want to do work that is in vain.

The passage then outlines what love looks like. "Love is patient, love is kind. It does not envy, it does not boast, it is not proud. It does not dishonor others, it is not self-seeking, it is not easily angered, it keeps no record of wrongs. Love does not delight in evil but rejoices with the truth. It always protects, always trusts, always hopes, always perseveres" (vv. 4–7).

You'll notice one thing Paul doesn't mention here. He doesn't say that "love means we agree all the time on everything." There is a fixed body of truth that Christians have believed for two thousand years, of course, which is why to another church, Paul said to be "like-minded" (Phil. 2:2). But we are talking about the ability to live with people who see lesser things in a different way than we do.

Paul offers some marks of Christian love:

- Patience
- Kindness
- Lack of envy
- Humility
- Respect
- Selflessness
- Self-control
- Keeps no record of wrongs
- Does not delight in evil
- Rejoices in truth
- Gives the benefit of the doubt (always believes, hopes, trusts)

We should ask ourselves, even in our most contentious fights, even when we think we are standing on principle in a dispute with another believer, whether we are embodying these virtues. Francis Schaeffer, one of the most important thinkers in the twentieth century, who was unflinching in his apologetic for the Christian faith, nevertheless warned believers to check their motives during conflict. In his book

The Mark of a Christian, Schaeffer wrote, "The world must observe that when we must differ with each other as true Christians, we must do it not because we love the smell of blood, the smell of the arena, the smell of the bullfight, but because we must for God's sake."[5]

Schaeffer is getting at our motivations. There is a difference between courage unwilling to back down from important conflicts and a sinfully quarrelsome spirit that lacks love. In the midst of a worthy fight with the church at Corinth, Paul stops and outlines what a heart of love looks like:

- *Does not delight in evil.* How do we react when we hear a church member's sin, when the whispers happen to be true, when our dislike of another Christian seems to be vindicated? Do we pump our fists? Do we project an air of triumphalism? Do we revel in the fact that someone else is engaging in sin and making us look good? Do we post something self-glorifying on social media? Love grieves, rather than rejoices, at evil and resists the gotcha tabloid mentality that traffics in gossip and looks to make other Christians look silly.
- *Rejoices in truth.* Just as we shouldn't delight in someone's downfall, we should be quick to praise what is true and good and beautiful. Love *rejoices* in truth. This also means that love works to separate the true from the untrue. Spreading lies or half-truths demonstrates a lack of love.

- *Love believes all things.* Christian love toward each other gives the benefit of the doubt. It doesn't automatically assume malice. Erik Raymond says it like this: "To 'believe all things' means that we give others the benefit of the doubt. It means that we expect the best. It means that we are able to overlook the offences and failure of others. It means we believe that over time we can commit ourselves to one another. 'Believing all things' means that we are willing to trust one another."[6]

This is one significant way we can show our love toward our brothers and sisters in this digital age, when rumors, untruths, and false accusations fly at twice the speed of truth. Social media offers no benefit of the doubt, which is why Christians should be the first to demonstrate it to show an otherworldly, Christlike love.

Enriched by Love

Love is not merely a command. It is also a gift. When we open ourselves up to the kind of love we've described, it gives us an opportunity to grow in our love for God. Firestone and Pierce again speak of the spiritual benefit: "Christian friendship plays a central role in the sanctification of the individual believer."[7] I've found this to be true in my life. I've found conversations with other Christians to be among the most important pathways toward spiritual health. This is especially true of Christian friendships with people who might not see everything the way I see things.

Right now, I have a friend to the left of me politically who constantly texts me when he thinks an article I've written or a tweet I've posted is probably a bit too, shall we say, conservative. And we go back and forth. But I always try to end it with something like, "You know, you really made me think. I'm thankful for you." I really am thankful for him. I also have a friend who probably thinks I'm a little too moderate for his taste and likes to text me and tell me what I'm not seeing. And I must tell you that I love this man and think of him as a dear friend and am thankful for his willingness to engage with me.

There is value in having friends that other people think are crazy. There is value in having friends that make others wonder why you even still hang with them. To love is not just to love those who think like us in every way. To love is to love when it's hard and annoying.

When John says, "You must also love your brother and sister," let's remember who he is talking to: a church increasingly diverse, a mix of Jews and gentiles, of people from around the known world, with clashing cultures and languages and customs. There was every cultural incentive for them not to get along.

The love that binds us as brothers and sisters should look a bit crazy and radical. It should be said of us, "Why are you friends with him or her?" It seems impossible or a bit naive until we consider how Jesus loves us. He loves us even though we're often unlovable. He loved us before we loved him (1 John 4:19), while we were still sinners (Rom. 5:8). We don't have to go very far to find an unlovable Christian. We only have to look in the mirror. I think of the moments in my life when I was the most ashamed of who I was, when I've embarrassed myself, when I've felt completely stupid. Jesus loved me in that very moment. All he is asking is that we extend that same love, love that the Spirit empowers in us (Rom. 5:5), toward others.

Perhaps we fail to love our brothers and sisters in Christ because we've forgotten how much Jesus loves our brothers and sisters. Jesus doesn't just put up with the church or tolerate the church. The Bible uses the language of marriage to describe our relationship to Jesus (Eph. 5:21–33; 2 Cor. 11:2; Rev. 19:7–9). This is a wedding between the one who is perfect and a bride whose sins were so heinous it required the ugly and unjust crucifixion of the Son of God.

Jesus isn't at all ambivalent about his feelings for Christians. Jesus is infatuated with Christians. I know how I felt at my wedding. I wasn't there merely because I tolerated Angela. I wasn't there because it was a business arrangement. I was there, standing nervously in my tuxedo, because I love Angela and wanted to be united to her for the rest of my life.

Jesus feels this way about the church. He feels this way about Christians who have been redeemed by his blood. Christ doesn't just tolerate his bride. He doesn't just sit next to his bride with an obvious eye roll. He isn't embarrassed by his bride.

Now think of that when you think of your fellow

Christians. I can think of two handfuls of Christians right now who I think (know) are totally ridiculous. So ridiculous I don't want anything to do with them. But here's the funny thing, the wild thing: Jesus wants everything to do with them.

Sometimes you are the one who is ridiculous. You are on someone else's naughty list. And guess what? Jesus isn't rolling his eyes at you either! He loves you too.

Christians are empowered to love one other by God's love for us, but we are commanded to love one another because this is the primary way in which an unbelieving world is attracted to Jesus. This is what Jesus tells us in John 13:35: "By this everyone will know that you are my disciples, if you love one another." Francis Schaeffer writes again about how important this is: "If the world does not see this down-to-earth practical love, it will not believe that Christ was sent by the Father."[8]

If we desire to fulfill the Great Commission, to see people who are far from Jesus come to know him in the way that we know him, if we want the world to put their faith in the one who died, rose again, and is coming again to renew and restore the world, love for our fellow Christians is one of the most visible ways we witness. Megan Hill, author of *A Place to Belong: Learning to Love the Local Church*, writes, "We cannot make anyone lovely—not in the way that God does by removing our sin and imputing Christ's perfect righteousness to us. But our love for one another in the church does produce a sort of radiant loveliness that shines before a watching world."[9]

Practices of Love

So what are some practices that can demonstrate this radiant loveliness? Here are a few things I've seen in people who best embody what Schaeffer calls "visible love."

Be willing to say I'm sorry. In our families, in our homes, in our churches, online, and anywhere else we interact with others, too often we cause hurt, either intentionally or unintentionally, and we allow pride to keep us from asking for forgiveness. Schaeffer says this:

> This is the way of renewed fellowship, whether it is between a husband and a wife, a parent and a child, within a Christian community, or between groups. When we have shown a lack of love toward this other, we are called by God to go and say, "I'm sorry. I really am sorry."
>
> If I am not willing to say "I'm sorry" when I have wronged somebody—especially when I have not shown him love—I have not even started to think about the meaning of a Christian oneness which the world can see.
>
> The world has a right to question whether I am a Christian. And more than that, let me say it again, if I am not willing to do this very simple thing, the world has a right to question whether Jesus was sent from God and whether Christianity is true.[10]

I've found this especially liberating in my life and ministry. I've had to say sorry so often to my kids, to my wife, to my coworkers, to my church members, to people with whom I've interacted online. But this doesn't come naturally. I'm stubborn. I like thinking I'm right. I don't like apologizing. But I've come to see that a simple apology goes a long way to heal and restore relationships.

Overlook quirks and flaws that are annoying but not ultimate. "Love," Peter tells us, "covers over a multitude of sins" (1 Peter 4:8). He is, of course, referring not to abuse and deep offenses but to the little things about others that drive us crazy: the choir member who can't seem to get to the top of the note on the chorus, the sibling who thinks Bigfoot is real, the small-group leader who chews his gum loudly.

Peter tells us to "love each other deeply," and doing that requires overlooking the quirks that drive us batty. Paul later tells the Colossian church to forbear one another (Col. 3:13). To forbear is to accept the reality of someone else's brokenness and to understand that others will accept the reality of our own.

Encourage more than you rebuke. We will have times of conflict and struggle with other believers. Any time you get more than one sinner in a room together, you'll have conflict. You'll sometimes need to rebuke or receive rebuke. But what if we made it a practice to encourage ten times more than we scold? Be intentional about it. Send that refreshing email to your pastor. Text your teenage daughter a sweet compliment. Write a note to a favorite author. Do it every time the Spirit gives you that inkling of an idea.

And before you post publicly about someone, ask yourself whether you are being fair, whether you are being loving in your critique, and whether if you were in that person's shoes reading what you said, you'd think it was in good faith.

Choose accountability over suspicion. Christians need the accountability of community. The most important place for that is in a healthy Bible-believing and Bible-teaching church. But there is a difference between accountability and suspicion. Accountability comes from a place of love. This is what Paul tells young Timothy as he urges him to stand up for what is right. He reminds him that every confrontation must come from "a pure heart and a good conscience and a sincere faith" (1 Tim. 1:5). This is different from operating out of suspicion, assuming malice and bad faith, a kind of gotcha mentality that assumes the worst. The former is important for healthy Christian relationships. The latter leads to unnecessary division and hurt.

This list of practices isn't exhaustive, and it takes a work of God's Spirit to form in us the kind of love that reflects the love of Christ, but it's a project worth pursuing, to live as those who sticketh closer than brothers, so that the world will see Jesus by our love.

Chapter 2

The Blood-Stained Banner

Virtue: Peace

The church of the New Testament is the church of the undivided Christ.

—Timothy George and John Woodbridge, *The Mark of Jesus*

One of my favorite books is the narrative nonfiction story *Boys in the Boat*, written by Daniel James Brown. I first read it several years after a recommendation from a friend. I know almost nothing about crew, a sport that has never piqued my interest. Yet Brown's beautiful storytelling and the unmatched narration of the late Edward Herrmann made this a compelling audiobook listen from the very first sentence.

Boys in the Boat follows the lives of young men from the western United States in the 1930s. The times were tough: crippling economic conditions, the Dust Bowl, and the specter of a second world war. The boys hailed from working class families and worked their way through school at the University of Washington, where they were recruited onto the crew team by legendary boat designer George Pocock and coach Al Ulbrickson. Ulbrickson shaped these motley men into a surprise championship squad, upsetting more well-established and well-financed teams on the East Coast before going on to win a surprise gold at the 1936 Olympics in Berlin.

What drew me in to this book was not its vivid depiction of the physically and mentally demanding sport of crew but the way Brown describes the uncommon unity of this unlikely championship team. Nine young men from varied backgrounds put aside their egos and worked together for a common purpose.

Act Unified Because You Are Unified

Most of us don't wake up in the morning and think about unity, but we appreciate it when we see it, whether it's the perfect synchronization of Olympic crew, the silent symphony of a functioning automobile, or the spectacular sight of a winter flock of geese flying in V formation toward a warmer clime.

Unity is woven into creation, from delicate environmental ecosystems to the harmony of the human body's many interdependent systems. Many moving parts, working in concert, is what gets us up in the morning, gets us to work, and gets us home at night. When just one of these parts is not working, when there is a discordant note in our day, we feel it. A pain in our joints. An oil leak in the minivan. A natural disaster in our town.

The Bible speaks of this kind of togetherness in the way Christians are called to relate to one another. When we think of Christian unity, perhaps we don't often envision the seamless cohesion of an Olympic rowing team. Instead, unity hits our ears and sounds like something sappy and sentimental like a bunch of religious people holding hands in a weird circle around a campfire. Or like the formulaic schmaltz of Hallmark movies.

However, togetherness is an essential part of what it means to be a follower of Jesus. You may not have realized this, but the day you met Jesus—in a dorm room, in a church aisle, watching a church service online, at a friend's house—you not only were reunited to God as your Father, you became part of something new: "For we were all baptized by one Spirit so as to form one body—whether Jews or Gentiles, slave or free—and we were all given the one Spirit to drink" (1 Cor. 12:13).

At the moment of salvation, you joined the largest family in the world. This word from the apostle Paul was to a troubled church in the city of Corinth, one that had been riven by division and disharmony. Like a bone out of joint in an otherwise healthy body or a broken valve in a car or an out-of-tune instrumentalist in a symphony, this congregation was discordant. Paul pleaded, You are all brothers and sisters. You have been joined to each other and joined to Christ.

In one sense, the togetherness of Christians is not something we create but something God has already done in Jesus. Whether we recognize it or not, we are unified with Christ and unified with the people of God. This is what is symbolized at our baptism as we are plunged into the waters of death and as we rise again in newness of life. We are in Christ and we are also plunged into the worldwide communion of saints in heaven and on earth.

Listen to what Paul says to another congregation, in Ephesus:

Remember that at that time you were separate from Christ, excluded from citizenship in Israel and foreigners to the covenants of the promise, without hope and without God in the world. But now in Christ Jesus you who once were far away have been brought near by the blood of Christ.

For he himself is our peace, who has made the two groups one and has destroyed the barrier, the dividing wall of hostility, by setting aside in his flesh the law with its commands and regulations. His purpose was to create in himself one new humanity out of the two, thus making peace, and in one body to reconcile both of them to God through the cross, by which he put to death their hostility. He came and preached peace to you who were far away and peace to those who were near. For through him we both have access to the Father by one Spirit.

Consequently, you are no longer foreigners and strangers, but fellow citizens with God's people and also members of his household.

—Ephesians 2:12–19

The Bible says that before we met Jesus, we were "separate from Christ," "without hope and without God in the world." This is the condition of every human soul in a fallen world. But now, because of Jesus' sacrificial death and victorious resurrection, Christians not only are brought near to God but are unified with people from every nation, tribe, and tongue into the family of God. Through the cross, Jesus "put to death hostility," and redeemed sinners are now "fellow citizens with God's people and members of his household."

Every believer is part of God's big and growing new family. This is why Paul later urges Ephesian Christians to "make every effort to keep the unity of the Spirit through the bond of peace." Why? Because "there is one body and one Spirit, just as you were called to one hope when you were called; one Lord, one faith, one baptism; one God and Father of all, who is over all and through all and in all" (Eph. 4:3–6).

In plain English, the Bible is saying to followers of Jesus, brothers and sisters redeemed by Christ, "You are already unified, so act unified." Just as Christians, because of Jesus' death in our place, are already declared righteous before God (2 Cor. 5:21) and are now called to live up to what we are (Phil. 2:12), the united people of God are now called to live out our unity in our daily interactions with other Christians. This is what it looks like to walk worthy of our calling (Eph. 4:1).

One of the primary marks of a Christian becoming more like Jesus is the earnest, heartfelt effort to love their brothers and sisters. John Woodbridge and Timothy George, in their classic, *The Mark of Jesus*, write, "To be baptized in the name of the crucified and risen Christ means that we have acquired a new set of comrades. We now wear the same cross on our uniforms, and we march together under the same banner, the bloodstained banner of the Lamb. We are soldiers engaged in battle, but we must not direct our weapons against one another, but against the real Enemy who has come 'to steal and kill and destroy' (John 10:10)."[1]

We wear the same cross on our uniforms and march under the same banner. This identity we have—as the blood-bought, redeemed, rescued, and resurrected people of God—is why the New Testament is so adamant about the way we treat each other.

To "make every effort to keep the unity of the Spirit in the bond of peace." *Make every effort* means that loving other Christians, overlooking flaws, putting aside differences, tolerating quirks, forgiving, and so on are not just nice things to see happen. They are essential to our identity as God's people. This is why Jesus prayed to the Father about the church in John 17:22–23 "that they may be one as we are one—I in them and you in me—so that they may be brought to complete unity. Then the world will know that you sent me and have loved them even as you have loved me." Our unity as brothers and sisters in Christ is a way we show an unbelieving world that we are unified with Christ, who is unified with the Father and the Spirit.

"The unity of the church," Gavin Ortlund asserts, "is not an optional add-on—something we can get to later. . . . The church's unity is foundational to her identity and mission."[2]

I Am of Beth Moore, I Am of John MacArthur, I Am of Tony Evans

So does unity mean Christians should strive for a plain vanilla sameness? Do we all have to dress the same, have the same study Bibles, and listen to the same music?

No. Romans 12:2 makes this contrast, urging Christians, "Do not *conform* to the pattern of this world, but be *transformed* by the renewing of your mind" (emphases added). Sometimes rigid conformity seems religious. Many cults, even bizarre Christian sects, demand this, with similar haircuts, clothing, preferences, and so on. And in a way the culture, while preaching expressive individualism, seems to push people to conform to its patterns.

The way of Jesus isn't this way, where our distinctive gifts, personalities, and experiences are melded into a boring blob, but instead forms us into the authentic people God created us to be (Eph. 2:10).

The gospel offers something radically better than conformity. It offers transformation. Growing in Christ means becoming the version of ourselves God created us to be, with our unique gifts and talents and personalities.

God's design for the church is the "one new man" in a mosaic of redeemed humanity. Unity demands that while we have our differences and distinctions, we are united by our common salvation. One Lord, one faith, one baptism.

This cuts so much against the grain in today's highly polarized world, a world where we are increasingly sorting ourselves based on ever-narrowing traits. We find common cause with others based not on shared loves but on shared hatreds. We join parties and coalitions not because we have a common set of values but because we have a common set of enemies. The internet makes this a lot easier because we can find people who hate the same things we hate.

Sadly this is increasingly characteristic of Christians.

We seem to be forming tribes based not on genuine theological commitments but on narrowing tribal matters. For instance, though we may share a similar set of theological beliefs as a brother or a sister, and may even be part of the same denomination or the same church, we don't see each other as allies because of cultural or political differences.

This is not a new problem. This was happening with the saints at Corinth. This congregation had divided into four camps. There were folks who appreciated the rational legal mind of Paul. Others preferred the smooth oratory of Apollos. Still there were many who resonated with the earthy truth-telling of Peter. And there were some who prided themselves on not being tribal and being "of Christ."

Paul rebuked this so strongly: "Is Christ divided? Was Paul crucified for you? Were you baptized in the name of Paul? I thank God that I did not baptize any of you except Crispus and Gaius, so no one can say that you were baptized in my name" (1 Cor. 1:13–15).

Paul is pointing the members of this church to their shared baptism in Christ. We are baptized not in the name of our favorite Christian leader but in the name of Jesus. "To affirm the unity of the church is to affirm that there are not multiple, distinct groups that constitute separate peoples of God," Ortlund writes. "Jesus does not have a plurality of brides. He has one bride, and her unity is so important that it was among the intended aims of Jesus' atoning death."[3]

Today these temptations are alive and well. But we might replace the names. We might say, "I'm a devoted follower of John MacArthur" or "I'm a huge fan of Beth Moore" or "I'm a Tony Evans disciple." And while it's not bad to have a preference of speakers or mentors whom God might use to speak to us in a powerful way, it becomes disunifying and idolatrous when this kind of distinction or preference causes us to look down on other Christians or label ourselves and others in such a way as to cause unnecessary divisions.

We should remember that when the New Testament talks about unity, the first application is in churches to whom the apostolic letters were written. It is in a local church where disunity and division are often most acute and where the consequences of sinful conflicts are most felt.

If you've ever been in a church that endured a split or had significant conflicts, you know it can be discouraging, wearying, and destructive. I have talked to so many pastors in recent years who shared with me the pain of church disunity, almost always over cultural issues and preferences rather than fights over gospel truths. Families take sides, lifelong relationships are severed, and, most tragic, a church's witness in a community is shattered.

This friendly fire is empowered even more today in the age of the internet, when we are often shaped by our favorite voices. A few years ago I saw a church member post online lies about the Christian organization for which I worked. I confronted her about this, asking her why she didn't come and ask me whether the information alleged in the article was true, and she sheepishly apologized. I forgave her and we moved on. But stories like this happen every week in churches around the country.

If we take Scripture seriously, we should fight for unity in our congregations, refusing to engage in behavior, online or offline, that might hurt a brother or sister in Christ.

I also believe the words of the New Testament should shape the way we see Christians outside our local bodies. We should especially heed this in an age when we can easily go on social media and quickly blast other Christians who don't think quite like us. These platforms not only incentivize incivility, they tempt us with opportunities to display our self-righteousness. Like the Pharisee in the temple, daily we are enticed to declare, "I'm so glad I'm not like those other Christians" (Luke 18:11).

So what does it look like to love Christians who are different than we are? Is it unspiritual to have favorite Bible teachers whose work has helped disciple our faith? I don't think this is what Paul is getting at when he rebukes the Corinthians. You'll notice he doesn't say that it was wrong for some folks to resonate with Paul or for others to enjoy listening to Apollos. He doesn't say it's wrong for followers of Peter to be loyal to this favorite apostle. What he is condemning then and now is a fierce tribalism that elevates these preferences above our loyalty to Christ and his body.

This is so easy to do, isn't it? I'm a proud Southern Baptist and theologically reformed. I'm a political conservative and a patriotic American. I should not be ashamed of any of these affiliations, but I must remember that Christ's body is not divided and that I share a Christian family with folks who are much different from me. If my identity as a Calvinist is my most important loyalty, I'll be a divisive church member. If my identity is solely as a Southern Baptist who votes conservative, I'll be a divisive Christian leader. If, like Jonah, my allegiance to my country supersedes my citizenship in heaven, I'll quickly abandon the call of God to love the nations for the sake of the gospel.

I'm sure you have memberships and affiliations of which you are proud. It can be healthy to have preferences, convictions, even tribes if we keep them in proper perspective. Our distinctions are why the commands in Scripture to love one another are so potent. When we love, in spite of our differences, we show the world something otherworldly.

I grew up in a church context where we often saw ourselves as the only true church and almost every other church as compromising the gospel. We reduced the body of Christ to "us four and no more, and I'm not sure about you three." For a significant part of my life I assumed that Christians in other denominations and even some in the tiny association of churches I grew up in were compromising their faith because they weren't as devoted as we were.

I remember visiting my cousins every Christmas and thinking super-judgmental thoughts. They had the audacity to be part of a fellowship of churches that believed basically everything we believed but were less legalistic. As a young teen, I looked down on them because they visited movie theaters or listened to Bono. I even prayed for their "spiritual maturity."

It wasn't until I began to read a bit more widely and listen to some Christian voices outside my small world that I realized that the body of Christ is wider than my tiny circle. When I became a pastor, I cultivated a wider group of friends and mentors and began to see the beauty in the diversity of Christ's body.

I believe this diversity is evident in the New Testament. Even in the book of Revelation, when the Spirit rebukes the seven churches, he rebukes them for their various sins, but not for their distinctions. God didn't expect Christians in Ephesus to look exactly like Christians in Smyrna. While we are held together by "one Lord, one faith, one baptism," diverse groups of Christians everywhere add a richness and beauty to the mosaic of Christ's body.

I enjoy getting to know Christians who worship differently than me. I remember attending services in the deep jungles of India that featured music I hardly could understand. And yet I wept when I heard the translator deliver the same gospel words that have united Christians across the centuries. I trembled when the cup and the bread passed my lips. One Lord, one faith, one baptism.

It's common for some to point to the thousands of ways Christian churches organize themselves and to lament our divisions. And yet at their best, when churches hold to the core Christian truths that God's people have believed for two thousand years, our denominational divisions showcase the rich diversity of the body of Christ. I am a Baptist by conviction, but I'm grateful for the way Presbyterians have not let me lose sight of the bigness of God and for how Methodists have urged me down to the altar and onto my knees in prayer and how charismatics have not let me forget that the Christian life is lived in the power of the Holy Spirit. The black church teaches me how to persevere in the face of oppression, while Anglicans have given us rich liturgies. Catholic social teaching is a helpful guide in a complex world, and Lutheran theology reminds us, daily, of God's rich and undeserved grace. My own denomination has brought a high view of Scripture and an emphasis on the importance of separating the church and earthly power. And what can I say of the value of monks in monasteries and evangelists in storefronts and other expressions of a thousand Christian traditions? I'm glad my bookshelves are full of the riches penned by authors from confessions I have not joined. Just as a body of believers cannot function without the diversity of the gifts of individual believers living out their callings, so too the Christian traditions bring important emphases that together make up the tapestry of the church Christ is building.

We should not be ashamed if God has called us to a specific denomination or tradition. The body of Christ needs faithful Baptists and faithful Presbyterians and faithful Lutherans and faithful Assemblies of God and faithful Churches of God in Christ and faithful from every genuinely Christian denomination. Still, we should not hold our denominational affiliations so tightly that we cannot love and learn from brothers and sisters who see differently.

Of course, Christian unity can only ever be based on truth. Paul's appeal to unity in Ephesians 4 is based on "one Lord, one faith, one baptism" and is centered on the truth about who Jesus is and what the Scriptures reveal about him. Jesus' plea to the Father in John 17 is that his people would be one as he is one with the Father, and yet is in tandem with Christ's work to sanctify them in the truth. "The way true Christian unity cannot be purchased at the expense of theological integrity," write Timothy George and John Woodbridge, "the first premise of any dialogue among Christians of different denominations or theological commitments must be that unity not based on truth is not unity worth having."[4]

There is an unhealthy push for a kind of religious unity that sees Christianity as just one more option alongside religions like Islam or Buddhism or Hinduism, a unity that papers over the historic doctrines of the Christian faith. The prophets in the Old Testament warned the people of God against mixing the worship of Yahweh with worship of pagan gods, and Paul warned against syncretism in 2 Corinthians 6: "What harmony is there between Christ and Belial? Or what does a believer have in common with an unbeliever?" (2 Cor. 6:15).

Like oil and water on a road in a spring rain, truth and untruth don't mix. To the church in Galatia, which was in danger of mixing the beauty of the gospel with the error of the Judaizers, Paul said that even a little untruth can be devastating: "A little yeast works through the whole batch of dough" (Gal. 5:9). In a later chapter we will examine more thoroughly why holding fast to the truth of Scripture is a worthy fight.

We should also be aware that unity can be used as a weapon to avoid dealing with sin and corruption. When cases of immorality or abuse are raised in unhealthy church contexts, there can be a desire to avoid facing sin. This too is addressed by Scripture. The church at Corinth willfully overlooked one of their members' openly engaging in sexual sin and then bragged about how loving they were. Appealing to unity in this case was the wrong approach.

Paul again offered a rebuke and the same metaphor he used with the Galatians: "Your boasting is not good. Don't you know that a little yeast leavens the whole batch of dough?" (1 Cor. 5:6). Their toleration of sin threatened the health of this church, could have destroyed their Christian witness, and was the least loving way to deal with the sinning church member. Thankfully, by the time Paul wrote 2 Corinthians, he had to urge the church to welcome this member back into their fold because he had gone through a process of repentance and restoration.

I've been in environments where abuses of power were dismissed for the sake of unity even though there was a genuine problem. But we should remember that in the same letter where Paul urged God's people to love, he also urged them to deal swiftly with a member flagrantly living in sexual sin.

A right view of Christian unity doesn't condone abuse or corruption but works to uncover it and lovingly call fallen brothers and sisters to repentance. Sin is the enemy of unity, a catalyst for disunity.

But even when we are convinced there is genuine sin, we should proceed with humility, not with the smug satisfaction of being in the right. After all, we too have feet of clay; we too are frail sinners, sculpted but from dust. "If you think you are standing firm, be careful that you don't fall!" (1 Cor. 10:12).

Unity as a Posture

Ultimately, unity, like the nearly perfect synchronization of the 1936 Olympic crew team, is less of a set of guidelines and more of a posture. Over and over again the New Testament is exhorting God's people to shed our worldly impulses to be proven right, to own people, to puff ourselves up.

Whenever I post online about Christian unity or engage in a conversation about it, inevitably I'll hear Christians wonder whether I'm making too big of a deal about it, as if it's a kind of footnote in Scripture. But a Bible without the commands to love is a Bible full of holes. We've already worked through Jesus' prayer in John 17 and Paul's exhortations in Ephesians 4, but there are so many more passages in Holy Writ that urge Christians away from division and toward unity:

- "But avoid foolish controversies and genealogies and arguments and quarrels about the law, because these are unprofitable and useless. Warn a divisive person once, and then warn them a second time. After that, have nothing to do with them. You may be sure that such people are warped and sinful; they are self-condemned" (Titus 3:9–11).

- "For all of you who were baptized into Christ have clothed yourselves with Christ. There is neither Jew nor Gentile, neither slave nor free, nor is there male and female, for you are all one in Christ Jesus" (Gal. 3:27–28).

- "Who are you to judge someone else's servant? To their own master, servants stand or fall. And they will stand, for the Lord is able to make them stand" (Rom. 14:4).

- "I appeal to you, brothers and sisters, in the name of our Lord Jesus Christ, that all of you agree with one another in what you say and that there be no divisions among you, but that you be perfectly united in mind and thought" (1 Cor. 1:10).

- "Therefore if you have any encouragement from being united with Christ, if any comfort from his love, if any common sharing in the Spirit, if any tenderness and compassion, then make my joy complete by being like-minded, having the same love, being one in spirit and of one mind" (Phil. 2:1–2).

- "Now may our God and Father himself and our Lord Jesus clear the way for us to come to you. May the Lord make your love increase and overflow for each other and for everyone else, just as ours does for you. May he strengthen your hearts so that you will be blameless and holy in the presence of our God and

Father when our Lord Jesus comes with all his holy ones" (1 Thess. 3:11–13).

- "Flee the evil desires of youth and pursue righteousness, faith, love and peace, along with those who call on the Lord out of a pure heart. Don't have anything to do with foolish and stupid arguments, because you know they produce quarrels" (2 Tim. 2:22–23).

On and on the Scriptures go, urging, commanding, exhorting the people of God away from petty fights and toward spiritual unity in Christ. And it's not just the commands to oneness that should convict us but the way Scripture sees a divisive spirit as something Christ saved us from and a spirit of unity as something Christ saved us to.

The apostle John says that a sign of a sinful soul is hatred toward a brother or sister. "Anyone who hates a brother or sister is in the darkness and walks around in the darkness" (1 John 2:11). Galatians describes "discord, jealousy, fits of rage," and "factions" as "acts of the flesh" (Gal. 5:19–21). And yet the fruit of the Spirit is the opposite: "love, joy, peace . . . goodness . . . gentleness . . ." (vv. 22–23).

How often we get this twisted. We sometimes see the person who argues every single point as the one who is spiritually mature and the person who patiently endures the foibles of others as weak and lacking courage. Christians too often adopt the world's ethic.

Francis Chan in his book *Until Unity* wonders whether ignoring this clear teaching of Scripture might be evidence of a deeper spiritual problem: "If you find yourself apathetic toward the commands of God for unity and unconcerned with how this appears to the world, you might have a bigger problem."[5]

So important is this posture of unity in a believer that in both of the passages in the New Testament that list the characteristics for pastoral leadership, the Bible demands these traits:

- temperance
- self-control
- not quarrelsome
- respectability
- not overbearing
- not quick-tempered
- discipline

Now think about how we often choose Christian leaders. We rightly wonder whether they have teaching gifts and whether they are morally faithful, but do we ask our pastors and leaders to demonstrate a spirit of unity? Do we look for leaders who resist quarrelsomeness and are temperate in speech? I wonder how many pastors disqualify themselves simply by the way they interact online.

We should periodically ask, How do we compare against this list of traits? What the church needs today are spirit-filled, courageous men and women unflinching in their convictions about what matters and gentle and sober in their demeanor. Imagine, for a moment, how refreshing this would be in a world riven by increasing tribalism and hostility.

I find that reading these Scriptures about unity makes me tremble.[6] God really cares about this, so much more than we do. A disunifying spirit is the sign of a deeper spiritual problem. And yet I don't want to leave you at the end of this chapter in a state of despair, for all of us are guilty of allowing sin to keep us from loving our neighbors and thus loving God.

The good news is that as God's people, we can prevail in repentance upon God's grace poured out to us on Calvary. The Spirit of God can do a new work, tearing away the strongholds of anger and jealousy and fear that drive wedges between us and our fellow Christians.

I'm humbled by the way Chan confesses his own journey toward love. "I am guilty of having sowed discord. Even now, as I study all these passages about division, I am embarrassed by my lack of remorse. Only a redemptive God with grace beyond comprehension could be this patient with me and still use me to teach about unity."[7] Chan puts into words what I feel. I think back on all the arguments and fights I have had with brothers and sisters, the way I was convinced they were either wrong or unenlightened because they disagreed with me on an issue of miniscule importance. I nearly lost friendships over political elections. Imagine how foolish that must seem in heaven!

Thank God we don't have to stay divisive. He can rescue us from the sin of quarrelsomeness. We can work toward unity, but not in our own strength. It can become easy to despair of our tendency toward quarrelsomeness or look at the state of the church and wonder how God can even use such a divided people. Yet we regain our hope when we gaze up again at our crucified Lord, who took on our sins of the tongue and heart and offers us his righteousness in exchange. Dwelling on Jesus' love for me fills me with love for the family of God.

Until Jesus comes, we'll never be fully unified. Division in Christ's body has been an issue from the first century to the twenty-first, and our generation is no exception. Yet when we commit to "striving for unity in the bond of peace," we show the world a tiny glimpse of that day when we will join with the great chorus in heaven of people from every nation, tribe, and tongue gathered around the throne of God.

Central to living what love requires, and essential for spiritual unity, is the ability to forgive. Too often Christians misunderstand this important doctrine. In the next chapter, we'll explore what forgiveness is and what it isn't.

Chapter 3

Drinking Poison

Virtue: Forgiveness

As I walked out the door toward the gate that would lead to my freedom, I knew if I didn't leave my bitterness and hatred behind, I'd still be in prison.

—Nelson Mandela

I'll never forget where I was when

I opened my laptop and read one of the worst emails I'd ever received. My wife was out of town with our little children, attending to a friend who had just lost her husband to cancer. I was in my study in the small church I pastored in Illinois, and it seemed the world was closing in on me. The church that had trained me, ordained me, and sent me out was not only withdrawing their association but publicly, to folks I'd grown up with, shaming me. This was not because I'd been caught in some moral failure or because I'd abandoned Christian teachings. They were cutting me off because I had the audacity to consider a different ministry model from the model they preferred. The differences were over things so miniscule and petty that if I put them here, you'd scratch your head in bewilderment and wonder.

I was hurt and angry and alone. I felt betrayed by the people who had coached me, raised me, and once supported me. I was a young pastor with few networks of support and friendship. I wondered whether this was the end of my ministry. Had the call I felt in junior high, walking down that dusty aisle at camp, come to an end here, like this?

In that moment the song "Come to Jesus" (untitled hymn) began to play from among the thousands of shuffled songs on my iPod. (Yes, I'm that old.) I am not much of a crier, but I broke down and wept. I called a longtime friend, an older ministry mentor who knew my situation.

"Rich," I said, "maybe I should quit. Maybe they are right. I just don't know if I can go on."

Rich told me two things that are etched on my soul. First, he said, "Dan, if you quit, I will personally drive from Michigan to Chicago and kick your butt. You are not quitting."

Then his voice got serious and he said, "Dan, you are right and they are wrong. But I'm telling you, in this moment, you have to make the determination to forgive."

I liked the first part of what Rich said. I felt then and I feel now that I was in the right in this conflict. I liked his encouragement to keep going in ministry. What was a hard pill to swallow was his admonition to forgive. I didn't want to forgive. I was in pain. But Rich was right.

How Can We Possibly Forgive?

Forgiveness, on its face, seems absurd. And let's be clear about what I'm talking about when I talk about forgiveness. I'm not referring to petty slights, mild annoyances, and garden-variety offenses. That guy who cuts you off in traffic, that lame meme a friend posted on Facebook, your teenager's sharp attitude while walking out the door—these are not the hurts we are talking about. For those, we should, as Christians, learn to "forbear and forgive."

But what about the deep, painful, life-altering hurts?

That email was the first of many hard emails in a painful year and a half of church ministry in which I lost quite a few friends and was slandered and rejected by some who raised me. I will not pretend that I was able to skate past these hurts like nothing happened. I won't pretend that I was perfect in all my interactions. And I won't pretend that what I've gone through is even close to what many who have experienced abuse, betrayal, and trauma have endured. But I do know this: forgiveness, this otherworldly, uncommon, audacious form of love, is available to those who know God.

When I was reeling from betrayal, I found an anchor in what Scripture tells us about how to deal with our hurt, particularly in the story of Joseph.

Joseph was the favorite son in a family riddled with dysfunction. Joseph was the great-grandson of Abraham, patriarch of a new nation God was forming as part of his plan to show himself to the world and bring about redemption. His father, Jacob, was both a follower of Yahweh and a terribly flawed, scheming, passive husband and father.

While his older brothers toiled in the family business, Joseph was paraded around as the heir apparent, symbolized by a colorful coat. The brothers, bitter at their father for his favoritism, jealous of Joseph's position, conspired to nearly kill him before humiliating him and throwing him into an old well. Then they trafficked him to some merchants who brought him to Egypt as a common slave. Meanwhile the brothers lied and told their father that his favorite son was killed by wild animals.

We know the story, of course, but the violence and

deceit don't get easier to read the more familiar we are with it. The injustice leaps off the pages of Genesis as the epitome of the depravity of the human heart. And here is Joseph, who quickly went from a prince with dreams of greatness to a piece of property, a commodity in the world's most powerful country.

Yet throughout the narrative is Moses' reminder that "God was with Joseph." In the pit, on the bumpy ride over to Egypt, in the prison after being falsely accused, and, of course, in his unlikely ascension to power in Egypt.

Joseph's rags to riches story is inspiring, but what struck me in my pain, with Rich's words echoing in my ears, was the way, years later, a powerful Joseph who could have enacted retribution on the flesh-and-blood family whose sinful jealousy and rage caused him so much suffering said this: "You intended to harm me, but God intended it for good to accomplish what is now being done, the saving of many lives" (Gen. 50:20).

Don't miss what Joseph is saying to his brothers, decades after he was left for dead in the bottom of a well before being trafficked to merchants and sold as a slave. He refuses to soft-pedal the evil done to him: "You intended to harm me." Other translations render this, "You meant for evil."

We need to get something important out of the way here. Forgiveness is not being passe about evil. Brushing off deep hurts as if they didn't happen is not forgiveness. Sometimes people talk about forgiving and forgetting, but do you think Joseph forgot what had been done to him? Do you think Joseph saw his brothers and said, "You know that time you betrayed me and lied about me and tried to ruin my life? I totally forgot that."

Joseph wasn't letting his brothers off the hook. He wasn't saying that their actions were no big deal. No, he looked his brothers in the eyes and he said to them, "What you intended was evil." True forgiveness recognizes the depravity of evil.

And yet he makes a remarkable statement: "But God intended it for good." The Hebrew reads something like, "God superintended it for good." This here gives us the age-old paradox of both human responsibility and God's sovereignty. I must confess that after decades of study, I still don't totally understand how both of those things can fit together, but in the desert of my deepest hurt, this doctrine was like a spring of cool water.

Joseph could forgive because he trusted that God is sovereign over all things. God saw when Joseph was thrust deep into a used well. He saw when he was tied and bound like common cargo and hauled to Egypt. He saw when Joseph was falsely accused by Potiphar's wife. That realization gave Joseph comfort.

It gives me comfort. It means that sinful human beings can plot evil, but ultimately God is working the worst things for my good and for his glory. I don't totally understand it, but it gives me hope, it helps me sleep at night, it allows me to remember that we are living not simply in a world of chaos but in a world where God is in charge and ordering all things for his purposes.

This is the same message Paul is giving the church in

Rome, which was increasingly facing persecution for their faith. He says to them, "And we know that in all things God works for the good of those who love him, who have been called according to his purpose" (Rom. 8:28).

Sometimes this verse is trotted out as a trite attempt to wave away hurt. But if we truly understand God's heart, a Father who is with us in our pain, we find comfort in knowing that while our world might be spinning out of control, there is one who upholds all things "by his powerful word" (Heb. 1:3).

This is the same word Peter gave to the crowds at Pentecost: "This man was handed over to you by God's deliberate plan and foreknowledge; and you, with the help of wicked men, put him to death by nailing him to the cross. But God raised him from the dead, freeing him from the agony of death, because it was impossible for death to keep its hold on him" (Acts 2:23–24).

How can we forgive heinous acts done against us? We can look no farther than the cross, where the world's greatest injustice was committed against the Son of God. If the cross, that symbol of torture and humiliation, was no accident but God's plan to bring about our salvation, then we can see our lesser but still painful hurts as part of God's plan for our good and his glory.

Otherworldly, Unexplainable Forgiveness

Forgiveness isn't just something you do, it's a gift you receive. This is a principle Jesus shared with his disciples in Matthew 18. He told a story of a king who was settling accounts with those who owed him large sums of money. Those were the days before easy credit and bankruptcy laws and protections that keep debtors from cruel punishment. For most of human history, if folks had a significant debt, they could be put in debtors' prison and their families could be sold to pay down what they owed. This was the case with the desperate man who stood before the king in Jesus' parable. In an act of grace, the king forgave the loan.

So what did this newly freed debtor do, having been offered such a fresh and unexpected lease on life? Did he throw a party? Did he walk away humbled by the grace he received? No, his first action was to go find someone who owed him a debt, a miniscule debt compared with his own balance that the king just erased. Not only did this forgiven man demand repayment, he resorted to violence to squeeze this tiny bit of cash out of his debtor. So disturbing was this that his friends found a way to tell the king what happened. As a result, the king rescinded the loan forgiveness and the ingrate was thrown back into prison.[1]

Jesus' point in this lesson is simple: forgiven people forgive. Jesus could urge his disciples to forgive because he was looking ahead to the day when, badly beaten beyond recognition, naked and gasping for breath, he'd whisper out a quiet grace for those who put him on the cross: "Father, forgive them, for they do not know what they are doing" (Luke 23:34). He could tell his disciples to forgive because he was the king who forgave their enormous, catastrophic, impossible-to-shed debt. And this is how we can summon the strength, the will, the energy to forgive those who have hurt us.

Colossians puts it like this: "When you were dead in your sins and in the uncircumcision of your flesh, God made you alive with Christ. He forgave us all our sins, having canceled the charge of our legal indebtedness, which stood against us and condemned us; he has taken it away, nailing it to the cross. And having disarmed the powers and authorities, he made a public spectacle of them, triumphing over them by the cross" (Col. 2:13–15).

We forgive only in proportion to how much we understand God's forgiveness of us. When we realize how deep and grave and reckless is our sin against God, we grasp the depth of his grace and are able to extend that grace to others. Nothing committed against us—no matter how heinous and traumatic and hellish—compares to what we've done to God. This doesn't mean our pain is any less painful or awful, it just means that our offenses against God are that awful. The debt we owed God is like the United States national debt—$30 trillion and climbing—and the debts others owe us are like the sums debated in small claims court.

Forgiveness is supernatural. When you see a Christian forgive, you are seeing the application of God's radical forgiveness spilled out. One of the most poignant examples of forgiveness I've ever read comes from Corrie ten Boom, whose family was taken to the concentration camps at Ravensbrück for the crime of sheltering Jews during the Nazi occupation of Holland. She suffered unspeakable cruelties and watched her sister Betsie die at the hands of her captors. After the war, she toured the world telling their story, captured in the bestselling book and movie *The Hiding Place*. But her teachings on forgiveness were challenged when one night, after speaking in Munich, Germany, a guard from Ravensbrück approached her after her talk and, having told her that he was a guard where her sister died, where so many people were tortured and killed, asked for forgiveness. He had recently put his faith in Christ. She shares how hard this was:

And I stood there—I whose sins had every day to be forgiven—and could not. Betsie had died in that place—could he erase her slow terrible death simply for the asking?

It could not have been many seconds that he stood there, hand held out, but to me it seemed hours as I wrestled with the most difficult thing I had ever had to do.

For I had to do it—I knew that. The message that God forgives has a prior condition: that we forgive those who have injured us. "If you do not forgive men their trespasses," Jesus says, "neither will your Father in heaven forgive your trespasses." . . .

And still I stood there with the coldness clutching my heart. But forgiveness is not an emotion—I knew that too. Forgiveness is an act of the will, and the will can function regardless of the temperature of the heart.

"Jesus, help me!" I prayed silently. "I can lift my hand. I can do that much. You supply the feeling."

And so woodenly, mechanically, I thrust my hand into the one stretched out to me. And as I did, an incredible thing took place. The current started in my shoulder, raced down my arm, sprang into our joined hands. And then this healing warmth seemed to flood my whole being, bringing tears to my eyes.

"I forgive you, brother!" I cried. "With all my heart!"[2]

With all my heart. Otherworldly, unexplainable forgiveness, made possible only by Jesus. A more modern example happened in the summer of 2015 when after a racist gunman opened fire on worshipers at Mother Emanuel AME Church in Charleston, the survivors stunned the watching world by uttering these three words: "I forgive you."[3]

Corrie ten Boom and the members of Mother Emanuel Church show us what it looks like to forgive. What about you? Think of all the hurts and pains you or your family have endured. Is there room for otherworldly, unexplainable forgiveness in your life?

Radical, otherworldly, supernatural forgiveness is essential if we are to embody the love God requires of us and if we are to live and serve as bridge builders among his people.

What Forgiveness Isn't

The inevitable questions about biblical forgiveness arise. Does forgiveness imply we ignore issues of justice and restitution? Does forgiveness absolve the guilt of the perpetrator? Does forgiveness imply reconciliation?

It's important for us to understand what is demanded of us in forgiveness. Forgiveness is not the same thing as reconciliation, which requires two parties who are willing to come together.

Consider again Joseph's story. For a long time, when I read the narrative in Genesis, I could never understand why Joseph, as prime minister, put his brothers through what seems a cruel series of tests. If, as he says in Genesis 50:20, he held no bitterness against them, why make them go back and forth between Egypt and Canaan? Why hide the cup in the brother's bag? Why hold one of the brothers as collateral? What is going on here?

In this example I think we see in Joseph the difference between forgiveness—which releases our souls from bitterness—and reconciliation. Before Joseph could be reconciled with his brothers, he had to see that they had shed the petty jealousies and rage that had motivated them to commit their heinous acts of violence in the first place.

Were his brothers remorseful for their treatment? Listen to the way they talk among themselves, with Joseph overhearing: "They said to one another, 'Surely we are being punished because of our brother. We saw how distressed he was when he pleaded with us for his life, but we would not listen; that's why this distress has come on us.' Reuben replied, 'Didn't I tell you not to sin against the boy? But you wouldn't listen! Now we must give an accounting for his blood.' They did not realize that Joseph could understand them, since he was using an interpreter" (Gen. 42:21–23).

Clearly, the guilt they had carried for decades, the

dirty secret that had hung over their hearts like a weighted blanket, was now being exposed in the light of day. They understood that God was forcing them to confront their sin and appeal for forgiveness and grace. Here are the seeds of reconciliation.

And yet Joseph had to continue to test them, to see if their remorse would lead to repentance and new patterns. Clearly it did. Instead of being brothers who cared only for their welfare, these men now pled on behalf of their youngest brother, Benjamin. These were changed men to whom Joseph could trust his heart.

It's important for us to understand there are levels of engagement when we've been seriously hurt, not all of which are possible to achieve in this life. Forgiveness is the first and is basic. Forgiveness is the act of being released from the bitterness of our pain and entrusting payback and vengeance to the one who fights for us. "Vengeance is mine," God tells us (Deut. 32:35 NASB; Rom. 12:17–19 NASB). James reminds us that "human anger does not produce the righteousness that God desires" (James 1:20).

Forgiveness means we refuse to let that other person live in our heads rent free. Forgiveness means we refuse to work our hurt into every single conversation. Forgiveness means we don't let bitterness cloud our judgment. This is why my friend Rich told me I had to forgive. He was telling me this for my spiritual and physical health.

I've seen too many people destroyed by bitterness. And here's the thing: unforgiveness not only affects our own souls, its acid splashes onto our families, our friends, our coworkers. All those years ago I had to decide. Would I model forgiveness for my family and for the small church I was called to lead, or would I let bitterness color my life? I've been up close and personal with too many leaders—powerful, gifted, brilliant leaders—who never got over their hurts. It hurt their leadership, making them fearful, isolated, and untrusting. Then they unwittingly inflicted pain on others.

And yet forgiveness is only the first level of engagement with those who have hurt us. The next level is reconciliation. But this is often more complicated. In Joseph's case, it happened because his brothers also engaged and were willing to embrace repentance and restitution. This is not always possible. Romans 12:18 says, "If it is possible, as far as it depends on you, live at peace with everyone." *If it is possible, as far as it depends on you.*

Sometimes, many times, reconciliation is not available. I've had relationships where I've forgiven and God has brought to my heart and soul a measure of peace over time, but full reconciliation was not yet possible because there was not a reciprocal effort to make peace.

Sometimes forgiveness is used as a weapon, for instance, to force victims to drop criminal charges against their abusers. But this isn't what forgiveness is at all. Forgiveness doesn't erase the demands of justice, it merely takes the instruments of vengeance out of our hands and releases our perpetrators to "the Judge of all the earth" (Gen. 18:25).

There is a third level of engagement beyond reconciliation

that is even harder to achieve. This is trust. You can forgive and even be reconciled in relationship, but it takes a lot to earn trust. This happens in broken marriages, where one partner has violated the marriage covenant. The offended spouse might forgive her husband and even be reconciled, after counseling and repentance on his part. But trust—the ability to know that she won't be hurt again by the one who hurt her—that takes a lot of years and patience.

Consider when Joseph confronted his brothers in Genesis 50. This was decades after he'd forgiven them, after they were reconciled and living side by side in Egypt. Yet they still wondered, after their father, Jacob, died, whether Joseph was just waiting to enact his vengeance on them. They repeated their father's deathbed wish that Joseph would forgive them of their sins against him. They wondered. Joseph not only responded that he would not take action against them but he pledged to take care of them financially and materially. He even entrusted them to carry out his dying wish: to take his bones back to the land of his father.

This level of trust, beyond forgiveness, beyond reconciliation, is the fruit of years of faithful actions by both parties to restore confidence. Too often we collapse these three concepts into one. But while forgiveness can happen in any situation, we can't force reconciliation where it's not possible, and we should be wise about whom we trust.

THREE DIFFERENT CONCEPTS
forgiveness | reconciliation | trust

If the treasurer steals money from the church coffers, the church should forgive him, but that doesn't mean he should be restored to his former position, because he hasn't earned the people's trust to handle their money. Forgiveness also doesn't mean people who have abused authority or committed moral failures should automatically be restored to their former positions. Sometimes, after years of restitution, people deserve a second chance. But we should be careful who we put in positions of power again. Again, God's grace is free and unlimited for our failures, but God never guarantees a return to the stage.

I can say today that I've forgiven and am at peace with those in my life who have deeply hurt me. That is the fruit of God's gracious work in my heart. I carry no bitterness or ill will. And I can say that almost all of my relationships are restored. But there are some folks whom I still have a hard time trusting. That's okay.

Forgiveness as a Habit

When my friend Rich urged me to forgive, it began a process that I'm still working on today. I've learned that forgiveness is not a one-time event but an ongoing process. It's a habit, a lifestyle, a way of life.

Jesus told the parable of the unforgiving debtor as part of a response to Peter's question about the nature of forgiveness. How often, the precious young disciple queried, must I forgive my brother? We don't know who he was talking about, but clearly it was a deep hurt that didn't seem to go away. Peter thought he was doing well when he said that perhaps forgiving seven times was enough. He was likely thinking about the prophet Amos, who urged forgiveness three times. Peter doubled that and added one more and thought perhaps he was good. Jesus responded to Peter's math of addition with his own math of multiplication. Seventy times seven. That's 490 if you are smarter than a fifth-grader.

It wasn't until I'd experienced my own hurt and betrayal that I really grasped what Jesus was getting at here. He's not giving Peter a checklist, as if once he rounded the bend at 487 or so he could stop thinking about forgiveness. No, Jesus is saying that forgiveness is not a one-time event but a habit, a ritual, a liturgy.

Pain is difficult this way. Just when we think we've put enough time and distance between us and our wound, something reminds us and the scab is ripped off our hearts: a song on the radio reminding of a failed relationship, a familiar building that brings us back to the place of pain, the face of a former friend on Facebook or in the grocery store. And those feelings of anger and rage and hurt come flooding back. Again, we must travel back past our trauma to the cross and release, once again, our burden to Christ.

I can say, though, that this habit is healing. There were places I just couldn't go, scenes I couldn't drive past, without the memories flooding back. Some days I had to forgive multiple times. I remember one time, years later, when I thought my heart had moved on and then I ran into someone from the church who had hurt me so deeply and

I just couldn't bear it. It was too much. I had to ask the Lord for grace.

But I'm here to tell you that I recently attended the funeral of a family member and sat in the same auditorium where so many hurtful things were said about me more than a decade earlier, and I can report to you that the pain I once felt there is gone. I was able to hold my head up high, to talk to people from whom I'd been estranged. God filled my heart with love for them. He healed my pain. What's more, this experience helped build spiritual muscles so that the next time I experienced hurt and pain, I had the spiritual resources to approach my situation.

I'm not saying, of course, that our hurts are no big deal or that the trauma of our trials doesn't leave scar tissue. I am saying this: If you don't resist the work of the Spirit of God, you can find it in your heart to forgive. And if you forgive, you can find a peace that "transcends all understanding" (Phil. 4:7).

How do you know you are on your path to forgiveness? Well, for me it began with the ability not to wedge the hurt into every conversation and the ability to resist seeing everything in the world through the lens of my experiences. I've seen others unable to do this, and that chip on their shoulder, which seems so comfortable to them, becomes an ugly distraction to everyone around. God can help you move past your pain into hope.

This may not be your experience yet. Perhaps you are still in the winter of your wounds and forgiveness is a moment by moment experience. Perhaps it will take more prayer, more counseling with those who can help free your tangled heart. But I want to tell you that this is okay. Time doesn't automatically heal all hurts, but time plus the practice of forgiveness can. When those memories flood your mind and soul, take that pain to the one who bore it and drink deeply from Christ's fresh reservoirs of grace.

Chapter 4

Our Glorious Mess

Virtue: Joy

There is nowhere else on earth that you will be nearer to heaven.

—Megan Hill, *A Place to Belong*

Bad headlines about the church rain down, every day it seems. You can't escape them, from secular media outlets to Christian media outlets to texts from your small-group members to Facebook posts by your friends and family.

Some are infuriating:

- "Church Leader Embezzles Money"
- "Christian College Leader Confesses Affair"
- "Denomination Admits Covering Up Abuse"

Some are sensational hot takes:

- "Christians Are Abandoning the Truth"
- "Christians Don't Care about the Poor"
- "Christians Are Too Political"

Or perhaps you are more familiar with localized critiques:

- "No churches in this town preach the true gospel."
- "I can't find a church that has the courage to speak the truth."
- "Every church I go to is insulated and unfriendly."

Perhaps it's the way we get our information. Perhaps it's because we are all online so much, doom scrolling and sharing our opinions. Perhaps today we seem to know instantly about every scandal.

Whatever is driving our cynicism, it feels like dumping on the church is an increasingly favorite pastime. It's nearly a cottage industry: blogs, podcasts, YouTube channels, and other outlets dedicated to bringing fresh news of Christian failure. Every week another bestselling book describes the terribleness of evangelical Christians. (The author, of course, is always the exception.)

It has gotten to the point where saying something good about the church is almost, well, scandalous. Like if you post a story or if you say you love your church or fellow Christians, people look at you funny or online they'll dunk on you and tell you how wrong you are. It's so fun how the internet has brought us together.

This is not to say that our cynicism doesn't have roots in reality. There is way too much corruption and scandal among Christian leaders. There are too many Christians more willing to please their peers than to take up their crosses and follow Jesus. And not enough churches stand boldly on the Word of God while also being friendly and loving to their communities. We'd be lying, we'd be naive, we'd be ridiculous if we insisted that everything is fine in every Christian community.

And yet I'm afraid we are tempted, in this age, to be catechized by bad headlines, tabloid-style takedowns, and a jaundiced view of churches until we yield to cynicism.

In doing so, we not only lose our joy but miss the work the Spirit of God is doing among the people of God.

The Elijah Syndrome

One of my favorite verses in the New Testament is a bit of an odd one. James, writing about prayer and dependence on God, makes this statement: Elijah was a man like us (James 5:17).

Now, I've gone to church my whole life and have learned a lot about Elijah. He's the wild wilderness dude who called out a wicked king in Israel, Ahab, and his equally wicked wife, Jezebel. Think about this. To this day, in 2022, *Jezebel* is a euphemism for wickedness. There is even a trashy magazine with this name!

Not only did Elijah have the courage to call out wicked rulers—at a time when doing so usually meant you would die—but he challenged the false religious leaders of his day to a special kind of duel. He called down fire from heaven on Mount Carmel in an epic display of God's power. As a kid this was always a favorite story in Sunday school and vacation Bible school and summer camp. Elijah was an example of boldness and courage, almost like a Bible superhero. He even made flannel graph exciting.[1]

So when James says, "Yeah, Elijah was like us," I do a double take. I've built a nice bonfire in my back yard, but I've never called down fire from heaven. I've written some pretty snarky social media posts, but I've never stood in the court of a king who could cut my head off and told him he was wrong. I had to walk half a mile to the showers at camp, but I never lived in the wilderness like Elijah. I've prayed that it wouldn't rain, especially when we lived in Nashville, where rain is its own season, but I've never prayed a prayer that stopped all precipitation for three and a half years. So how is Elijah like me?

Well, to see the humanity of this superhero, we have to go to a passage of 1 Kings that is usually left off the flannel graph. Here, Elijah kind of does look like us. He's burned out. He's tired. And he's pretty cynical about the people of God.

You might say that if he had social media, he'd be complaining about being the one person standing for truth. Or he might be the person who stays home on Sunday because "no church is preaching the gospel right." Or he might be the guy at the office who grew up in church and now says that Christians are a bunch of hypocrites.

Elijah, in one chapter, has turned from prophet to cynic. Fresh off an epic battle where he called out the false prophets and God sent rain again after a famine, Elijah fled to the wilderness because Jezebel still wouldn't repent.

God's messenger is discouraged and defeated. He's weak and vulnerable. His heart is crusted over with layers of suspicion and contempt. "I'm the only one," Elijah complains to God. "I have been very zealous for the LORD God Almighty. The Israelites have rejected your covenant, torn down your altars, and put your prophets to death with the sword. I am the only one left, and now they are trying to kill me too" (1 Kings 19:14).

What's strange about Elijah here is that he has just come off a spiritual victory where he witnessed the power of God to move the hearts of Israel from idolatry to true worship. And yet all he can see is the one person in Israel who refuses to worship God: Jezebel.

Elijah was a prophet of God. Prophets are often called to do hard things, to stir up the people of God away from sin and toward righteousness. It's often a lonely task to say hard things. We need prophets in our day, gifted and godly men and women willing to say things that are hard to be said, to call out wickedness.

And yet there is a difference between being prophetic and being cynical. Prophets wrap hard words in hope. If you read Isaiah and Jeremiah and John the Baptist and Micah and others, you'll read rebukes, but you will also read words of hope and comfort, a path forward from sin to salvation. Cynics aren't interested in salvation or transformation. They're only interested in an endless self-loathing ministry of doom.

A prophet speaks to people he loves with tears. A cynic disdains the people he is called to confront. A prophet's desire is to see transformation. A cynic's desire is to bring attention to himself.

Today, cynicism is contagious. It has become a movement, a niche lifestyle, a way of being.

God's words to Elijah are sobering. "I reserve seven thousand in Israel—all whose knees have not bowed down to Baal" (v. 18). In other words, "Elijah, you are not the only one doing the right thing." In plain English, God is telling his servant to get over himself. What's more, God tells Elijah to get up and prepare to meet his successor. What a humbling moment.

God is telling this prophet that not only is he not the only one following Yahweh but also someone will come after him who will carry on his ministry. Elijah, by yielding to cynicism, lost his voice.

And so do we. We think we are telling it like it is to other Christians. We get up in the morning, look in the mirror, and see a spiritual hero. But God's word to Elijah and to us is this: "You are not the only one following the right path. I have many others. This is not about you."

Nonprophet Ministry

God's word to Elijah wasn't that God's people don't need prophetic voices. Throughout Scripture, we see the Lord raise up leaders to speak hard words to stir God's people away from sin and lethargy. In the Old Testament, the words of the prophets to wayward Israel are words we should read today and take to heart. And in the New Testament, Jesus and the apostles were unsparing in their denunciations of sin and calls to repentance.

And yet there is a way that prophetic words should be delivered. They are words designed to build up and not destroy and are to be delivered not with glee but with humility. Consider the way Paul urges young Timothy to engage the church with hard words. In the midst of his urging Timothy to be bold against the incursion of false doctrine and sin in the church (1 Tim. 1:3–11, 18–20), he is transparent about his own fallenness. Paul remembers that before he was the apostle who wrote much of the New Testament, planted churches around the world, and was persecuted for his faith, he was "once a blasphemer and a persecutor and a violent man." But "I was shown mercy," he writes of his conversion, and "the grace of our Lord was poured out on me abundantly" (vv. 12–14).

Paul's prophetic ministry was born of his brokenness, of his love for the people of God. He wasn't coming in hot, trying to score rhetorical points or speak hard words for the sake of speaking hard words. Paul resisted the urge to make himself the center of things. Writing to the church at Corinth, which was steeped in carnality and sensuality, Paul's spirit was of a humble, almost reluctant prophet: "And so it was with me, brothers and sisters. When I came to you, I did not come with eloquence or human wisdom as I proclaimed to you the testimony about God. For I resolved to know nothing while I was with you except Jesus Christ and him crucified. I came to you in weakness with great fear and trembling" (1 Cor. 2:1–3).

The apostle wasn't spoiling for a fight. His aim wasn't more notoriety but repentance and the building up of the people of God. Paul saw the church the way Jesus sees the church, as the bride of Christ. So even as he penned tearful letters of rebuke, he wrote from a place of love.

Today, loathing seems more in vogue than love. Some prophets are worth listening to, but I find much critical commentary on the church today to be dripping with disdain. And the digital algorithms on social media reward this negativity.

In my experience, when I write something positive about the church or about a local church, I get negative feedback. But if I write something critical about the church, especially a wide, sweeping condemnation (I am writing fewer of these lately), it almost always goes viral.

Ironically, I find that the Christians who fight each other the most in public seem to share a cynical outlook. Either these would-be Elijahs see themselves as mighty warriors for justice, rooting out racism and sexism and every other bad *ism* from among deplorable Christians, or they see themselves as righteous guardians of orthodoxy, more courageous than those soft compromisers. In their minds, the church is either drifting toward heresy or embracing injustice.

How much easier it is for us to lament, whether in our online discussions or in our conversations with fellow Christians, "the state of the church" than to talk about the good things God might be doing among his people. It's easier to think that every church in town is weak or doesn't preach the gospel or doesn't do enough in the community than to roll up our sleeves and get involved and to lift our eyes to see the Spirit at work.

There is little market for the reality that the church is both messy and beautiful, sinful and sanctified, wonderful and wayward. Pastor Jon Tyson said it best recently: "There is a fine line between the prophetic and the cynical. One brings needed critique, the other brings unneeded criticism."[2]

Messy and Beautiful

I was recently out to dinner with a journalist and two other Christian leaders. The journalist, a Christian, is working on a book on the state of evangelicalism with its many fissures and scandals and problems, and wanted to hear our perspectives. All four of us had been hurt in public ways in the last few years by betrayals and lost friendships. My three friends have been hurt in much more profound ways than I have. So I sympathized in so many ways with them regarding the ugliness and hurt they've seen.

But what struck me is how easy it was for our conversation to linger on what is wrong with the church. I felt almost heretical whenever I raised examples of God's people doing good work around the world: the missions endeavors in dangerous and closed countries, the on-the-ground relief efforts of many denominations after natural disasters and war, the quiet way many Christians go about their daily lives of faithfulness in cities and communities around the world.

I came home discouraged. But then I remembered the Southern Baptist pastor in Texas who sent me $1,000 when I lost my job in 2021. I remembered the people in my own church who volunteered to form relief teams when tornadoes hit our state. I remembered the Sunday school teachers who nurtured my faith when I was a child.

Were the experiences of my dinner companions real? Yes, these leaders had seen, like me, the dark underbelly of the church. And yet I'm afraid that an inability to see any good—to let the headlines, the bad stories, the corruption we've witnessed be the only story—is to suffer from the Elijah syndrome in 1 Kings 19. I'm not suggesting we pretend away the darkness. But I'm finding that the temptation toward cynicism is as toxic as naivete. It is to see the church through a simplistic frame.

Some people, however, are committed to going against this grain and working to highlight not just merely the scandal but also the stories of sacrifice and generosity. My friend Sarah Zylstra,[3] a journalist for the Gospel Coalition, chases these stories relentlessly. Recently I read about a Presbyterian church in Virginia who helped settle refugees from Burundi,[4] and about faithful missionaries who are bringing the gospel to Albania, an atheist country,[5] and about a doctor in Cape Town, South Africa, doing pioneering research on a malaria vaccine.[6]

I texted Sarah and asked her what motivates her to tell these stories. She sent me this:

> I am firmly convinced that Christian journalists have an edge on every secular journalist. To understand that God made the world, that it fell into sin, that Jesus redeemed it on the cross, and that we are working with him toward its restoration is an enormous advantage to understanding current events.
>
> It's also really freeing. I am not bound to look just at what is happening in Washington, DC. I can find the truer stories, which are almost always happening elsewhere.

When you read a history of the world, Israel is a tiny footnote, if it's noted at all. It just didn't impact world events in a big way. But if you look at God's story, Israel is in the central role.

I'm looking for that story—or those stories—the ones that aren't in the headlines but are carrying along the true narrative of humanity.

And they are good stories, where God is at work in amazing ways. They are gritty and raw, but also deeply hopeful and uplifting.

Notice that Sarah says these stories are both "gritty" and "raw." To see the good, to resist cynicism is not simply to act as if everything in the church is unicorns and fairy dust. Sarah's work is compiled in a book coauthored with Collin Hansen, *Gospel Bound: Living with Resolute Hope in an Anxious Age.*[7] I urge you to put this book down now and go pick that one up, especially if you are tempted toward cynicism. What I love about their work is that it doesn't sugarcoat or whitewash problems in Christianity. It doesn't soften theological convictions. But it does take our eyes off the relentlessly negative, the constant drumbeat of scandal and tabloid, and helps us to see that the Spirit of God is alive and active in the world today.

To see the church this way is not naive but realistic. It is to see the church the same way God sees the church, whether it's your local church or the worldwide church.

The New Testament in many places tells us that every Christian is a member of Christ's body, which means we are connected not only to Jesus but also to each other. Consider this passage in Romans: "For just as we have many parts in one body and all the body's parts do not have the same function, so we, who are many, are one body in Christ, and individually parts one of another" (Rom. 12:4–5 NASB).

Perhaps it's hard for us to think of being the body of Christ as a positive, given how, in a fallen world, we are often ashamed of our bodies. As we get older, that glance in the mirror after a shower is not a pretty sight. And yet Jesus is not ashamed of his body, because when he looks, he doesn't see the imperfections and sins that put him on the cross, but he sees the sanctified, washed, and perfect body we will be when he returns to take us home. So when we relentlessly dog other Christians or churches or organizations, when we malign each other, when we give in to cynicism, we are telling Jesus we don't like his body.

But not only are we described as Jesus' body, we also are portrayed in Scripture as Jesus' bride. Here is just one example: "Christ loved the church and gave himself up for her to make her holy, cleansing her by the washing with water through the word, and to present her to himself as a radiant church, without stain or wrinkle or any other blemish, but holy and blameless" (Eph. 5:25–27).

Not only is Jesus not cynical about the church, he is infatuated with the church, so much so that he loves the church and gave himself for her. That's right, Jesus is beaming with pride over his bride. What about the sin and corruption and selfishness we often see from Christians or that we often display? What about the churches that are compromising the gospel or that are not serving their neighbor or that are beset by scandal or corruption?

Jesus loves those Christians too. And remarkably, Jesus doesn't see his bride for all of her imperfections—though there are many—but sees her—us—as a radiant bride. This is our future:

> Let us rejoice and be glad
> and give him glory!
> For the wedding of the Lamb has come,
> and his bride has made herself ready.
> Fine linen, bright and clean,
> was given her to wear.
>
> **—Revelation 19:7–8**

This is how God sees his people. This is how Jesus sees his bride. And this is how we should see ourselves and our fellow believers.

In her book *A Place to Belong: Learning to Love the Local Church*, Megan Hill reminds us that it's not as if New Testament authors such as Paul were naive about the problems in the churches:

Paul [experienced] many of the challenges of life in the local church. He was viewed with skepticism by church leaders (Acts 9:26). He suffered personal attacks from false teachers and their disciples (2 Cor. 10:10). He was intentionally misunderstood by other Christians (2 Pet.

3:16). He had disagreements with other Christians (Acts 15:36–40). He was disappointed by other Christians (see 2 Cor. 11:22–29). He sat alone in prison, longing for committed fellow workers but realizing "they all seek their own interests, not those of Jesus Christ" (Phil. 2:21). And—in what may be the saddest verse in all of the Epistles—he recounts, "At my first defense no one came to stand by me, but all deserted me" (2 Tim. 4:16). If anyone knew how disappointing the local church can be, it was the apostle Paul.[8]

The local church and the worldwide church can be disappointing. I have church people in my life who have hurt me. I am sure you do too. The apostle Paul did. He even named them in many of his letters. And yet this reality didn't deter Paul from urging God's people to rejoice, to resist cynicism. Hill writes again: "Christ is not the powerless head of a terminally ill body. . . . Christ will make his whole body holy just as he is holy."[9]

This is why the common phrase "I love Jesus, but not the church" is problematic. If Jesus is the head of the church, if the church is his body, it's hard to imagine a scenario where it's possible to love Jesus fully without loving his church deeply. In a sense, this is like telling Jesus we love him but think his body is grotesque. That's like telling Jesus we like him but think his bride is ugly. That's telling Jesus that the people for whom he died are not worth our love, even though we are among those people we think are not worth loving.

To hate the church, to be cynical about God's people, to see only the blemishes is not only to hate Jesus but to hate ourselves, for if we are believers, if we are blood-bought and redeemed Christians, we are connected to other Christians and connected to Christ.

I realize you may be reading this in a season of pain. Your church or some fellow Christians might have recently hurt you. If that's the case, please know that I'm not suggesting that justice should not be satisfied or that trust should automatically be restored. But I am suggesting that the universal body of believers—the church—is something Jesus finds beautiful, and so should we.

The Cure for Cynicism

Those nasty headlines, the news of yet another Christian leader falling, the fallout from yet another church split—those will be with us in every generation of the church until Jesus returns. The Jesus movement was not even a century old before scandal (Corinth), apathy (Ephesus), and compromise (Laodicea) were problems.

The solution to our cynicism, then, is not to look away from the church's many blemishes, to pretend they don't exist, to whitewash history where the church has been complicit in evil but to recognize that the church's goodness is not in herself but in the one who redeemed her.

This is why Paul urged the church at Colossae to "Set your minds on things above, not on earthly things" (Col. 3:2). Dustin Benge writes, "Have you given up on the church? Shift your gaze from your hurt and disappointment and behold the church through the eyes of Christ. Behold her through the lens of Christ, who willingly died in her place and rose from the dead to secure her eternal life. When you see the church—not for what she does, but for who she is—perhaps, in time, you too will proclaim, 'you are beautiful.'"[10]

Which brings us back to Elijah. I find it compelling that one of the ways Jesus helped restore his prophet was to give him an assignment. Elijah was to anoint his successor, Elisha. Not only was this a rebuke to the myopic "I'm the only one doing it right" but it was a fresh injection of hope into a weary soul. We are not better than Elijah, the one who called down fire from heaven at Baal, who appeared by Jesus' side with Moses on the Mount of Transfiguration. No, Elijah was a man like us, according to James, but we are like him in that disappointment can harden into a crust of distrust around our souls.

Perhaps a way to get a fresh vision of Jesus' love for the church is to, like Elijah, look and see what God is doing among the generation who will come after us. Elijah saw a prophet who not only was endowed with the same Spirit who gave him power but would have a "double portion" (2 Kings 2:9) of God's blessing. God's word to the prophet who would be carried to heaven in a flaming chariot, who prophesied the deaths of Israel's wicked monarchs, who appears at the end of the age in the book of Revelation was that the one who was to come after him would be even more effective than he.

Not only are you not the only one standing for truth, not only are you not the only one resisting the spirit of the age, not only are you not the only Christian doing it right, but there is also a generation coming after you who might be even more faithful than you. This stirred Elijah and he went on to guide Elisha into the next season of ministry, and then he was carried home by the Lord.

I don't know how this chapter is reaching you today. Perhaps you are deeply cynical about your church, the worldwide church, evangelical organizations, or your particular denomination. Maybe, like my dinner companions, the hurt and pain have clouded your vision of Christ's beautiful body. If so, I invite you to step away from your cynicism and see what God might be doing in the world, perhaps even among the next generation.

How can we restore our joy? When I'm tempted toward cynicism, I return to a passage of Scripture Peter wrote to a discouraged people: "But you are a chosen people, a royal priesthood, a holy nation, God's special possession, that you may declare the praises of him who called you out of darkness into his wonderful light. Once you were not a people, but now you are the people of God; once you had not received mercy, but now you have received mercy" (1 Peter 2:9–10).

Let's remember who we are and whose we are. And we might periodically ask God to examine our hearts to see what our real aim is when we proffer criticism of our church, of the church at large, of other Christians. Is it to build up the body of Christ or bridge divides? Or do we just want to score a few cheap points to be proven right? Prophetic words are meant to build up, but cynical words tear down. Prophets rejoice in repentance; cynics won't allow themselves to see renewal.

Loving as Jesus loved means we are not naive about sin in the church but are always eager to see the good among God's people. One way to start is to pick up a book like *Gospel Bound* and read about the work of faithful believers around the world. Or maybe it's time to find a younger believer who is full of zeal and passion whom you can mentor and disciple. Let's gaze up and away from the headlines toward that vision when Jesus returns to take his bride, resplendent in glory, home.

God refocused Elijah's gaze on the small, the obscure, and the seemingly insignificant, those quiet places where the Almighty is at work. And so that is a practice we might pursue. This is what we'll look at in the next chapter, a fresh approach to faithfulness in an era of Christian celebrity.

Chapter 5

Christian Famous

Virtue: Humility

The soul was made to stand in awe of a Person—the only person worthy of awe. All heroes are shadows of Christ. We love to admire their excellence. How much more will we be satisfied by the one Person who conceived all excellence and embodies all skill, all talent, all strength and brilliance and savvy and goodness.

—John Piper, *Don't Waste Your Life*

About fifteen years ago,

Angela and I were serving at a small church where I was the volunteer youth pastor. It was our first month, and one Wednesday night we chose an icebreaker game where the names of famous people were pinned to the back of every guest and they had to ask a series of questions to figure out who they were. One young kid got what I assumed would be one of the easiest assignments. The sign on her back read "Billy Graham."

Yet I was stunned—and remained stunned all these years later—that neither this young teen nor her dozen or so peers knew the man who may have spoken to more people than any preacher in history, who was a regular at the White House for every president from Truman to Trump, whose presence was ubiquitous across media for almost three-quarters of a century.

She didn't know who Billy Graham was. I couldn't believe it. It was a stark reminder that even the most famous Christians are not as famous as we think and of how fame, if we achieve it, can be fleeting. The most significant people in one generation will most likely be forgotten by the next.

To his credit, Billy Graham accepted his calling to be an evangelist, sharing the good news of the gospel around the world, but was never really all that comfortable with his fame. In 1989, he was the first preacher ever to receive a star on the Hollywood Walk of Fame. When asked about this honor, he replied, "My primary desire today in having my name inscribed upon this Walk of Fame is that God would receive the glory. I hope someday somebody will come and say, 'Who is Billy Graham? What did he stand for?' Perhaps a child will ask his parents or grandparents, and they will tell him that he was not a celebrity, not a star, but a simple preacher of the Gospel. And that they might explain the Gospel to him, and that many might find Christ in that."[1]

What a refreshing perspective, perhaps one that we might consider for ourselves, whether we preach to thousands or nobody outside of our hometown ever knows our name, whether our gifts put us up on stage or keep us back in the kitchen washing dishes.

The Age of the Stage

Billy Graham's discomfort with fame is a needed refresher in an era when fame—the fifteen-minute variety purchased so easily today—is all the rage.

In a recent survey of thirty thousand kids in the United States and the United Kingdom, young kids ages eight to twelve were asked what they want to be when they grow up. The majority, 56 percent, said they want to be a famous YouTube star. Not an astronaut or a lawyer or a doctor. I'm afraid we live in an age when the lure of celebrity has never been stronger.

Of course there is nothing inherently wrong with being a YouTube star. My teenage son absolutely loves watching Dude Perfect and Mr. Beast and other wholesome entertainment. Many of these online celebrities are Christians using their platforms to be agents of grace in a hurting world. And yet there is something a bit discomfiting in the way a rising generation aspires first to the vocations that are the most public. Could it be this insatiable desire came from watching adults—us—seek their own shortcuts to glory? This is the intoxicating drug of our age, promising instant validation, a platform, and an audience. This is why we have such a hard time—not just kids but adults too—tearing ourselves away from the devices in our pockets. One expert says it this way: "The largest industry in the world now is quite literally the attention-seeking industry. This industry is driven not by what we do, but by the information extracted from us."[2]

The desire to be known is not just an "out there" problem but a motivation for many followers of Jesus. We are tempted to use our gifts and talents not to bring glory to God and grace to our fellow believers but as ways of elevating ourselves. It could be as big as angling for a few thousand more followers on our favorite social-media platform or as small as elbowing our way to the stage in our churches. The Bible's warning not to "think too highly of ourselves" was delivered to a church the size of your small group.

The impulse to bring glory to ourselves is as old as the sun. Jesus' own disciples, plucked from the obscurity of their ordinary lives, tried to muscle their way into Jesus' inner circle. Two brothers, James and John, even enlisted their mother to ask Jesus if, in the coming kingdom, they could have prominent appointments.

Jesus' response was that the brothers didn't really know what they were asking for. To touch that inner ring would not involve pomp and circumstance, power and privilege. Instead, to be close to Jesus demands self-denial and suffering, taking up a cross: "When the ten heard about this, they were indignant with the two brothers. Jesus called them together and said, 'You know that the rulers of the Gentiles lord it over them, and their high officials exercise authority over them. Not so with you. Instead, whoever wants to become great among you must be your servant, and whoever wants to be first must be your slave—just as the Son of Man did not come to be served, but to serve, and to give his life as a ransom for many'" (Matt. 20:24–28).

Jesus' words are as relevant today as they were to the disciples who first heard them. To be genuine agents of grace, Jesus is asking his followers to put aside the need to be a big deal. Of course, misplaced ambition is a hard thing to identify in ourselves. It's easier to spot in others. How do we know we are trying too hard to seek attention, find an audience, hold a position? Those of us who work in public spaces must constantly check our hearts. I've been a public person for most of my career as a writer, preacher, and speaker. My calling requires an audience. To prepare a sermon, to write an article, to accept a speaking engagement supposes that I have a message worth sharing. So how do I know, how do any of us know, when we are merely stepping into our callings and when we are guilty of seeking fame for fame's sake?

I don't think Jesus is discouraging public ministry. Having a platform isn't wrong. The apostles Jesus is speaking to here about leadership went on to preach to thousands at Pentecost. They preached the gospel around the Roman Empire and authored, under the inspiration of the Spirit, the New Testament that we hold in our hands. We name our kids and our towns and our churches and our hospitals after these people.

In every generation, God raises up men and women for public ministry, some as preachers and teachers in the church. Some, by virtue of their callings, are put in positions of power and fame. Those positions aren't wrong. God used wealthy and powerful men like Abraham and Job. God raised up political leaders like Daniel and Joseph and Esther. Today there are some famous Christians in professional sports, business, and the arts. Should they all abandon these posts to avoid being celebrities?

I don't think so. At times Scripture encourages public ministry. God rejected Moses' resistance to leadership and urged Joshua not to shrink from his calling. Not only does Paul call Christian leadership positions a gift to the church (Eph. 4:11–13), he encourages Timothy not to neglect his calling (1 Tim. 4:14) and writes that stepping into a public position of leadership is a good thing (1 Tim. 3:1).

I for one am grateful that God raises up people with big public platforms. Because Billy Graham's sermons were on television and because he held massive crusades, his preaching of the gospel came around to my father and then it came to me. Because of preachers on Moody Radio in my hometown, I was discipled in my car by people like Chuck Swindoll and Alistair Begg and Tony Evans. Because C. S. Lewis was popular and his books have circulated around the globe, his Chronicles of Narnia series and his book *Mere Christianity* helped strengthen my faith. I'm grateful Charles Spurgeon was famous because I get to read his sermons. I'm glad Tony Dungy, a former NFL football coach, uses his public platform to proclaim Christ. His books on leadership have helped me tremendously. I'm glad I can listen, as I write, to hymns sung by country music star Carrie Underwood.

So as I warn about the temptation toward raw ambition and seeking fame, I don't want us to think that a position or a platform is inherently bad. But what Scripture is constantly getting after and what all of us—whether famous, infamous, or obscure—must consider is that the satisfaction and joy we can find in the size of the crowd are fleeting.

A Fleeting Satisfaction

Pride tempts all of us whether we have thousands of followers online or teach a Sunday school class of twenty people. Within each of us lies the disordered desire for fame: the pursuit of power for the sake of power, the pursuit of wealth for the sake of wealth. Pride doesn't afflict only young kids who want to be YouTube stars. It afflicts people in churches who fight and claw for a position on an important committee. It afflicts employees who use gossip and underhanded tactics to get a promotion at work. It lies beneath the use of anger to build an online audience.

If we are following our callings as the people of God, it could be that hard work and obedience to Christ give us a public platform. But we should always hold it loosely, seeing leadership not as a way to enrich ourselves but as a way to serve others. We might say with the writer of Proverbs, "Give me neither poverty nor riches" (Prov. 30:8), or like Paul be content whether being humbled or having abundance (Phil. 4:12). This is what Jesus is getting after. He didn't rebuke the disciples because they sought positions of leadership. He rebuked them because of what they intended to do with their leadership.

I think back often on that night in youth group so many years ago and it reminds me that while God does raise up prominent Christians and spiritual heroes—people with extraordinary gifts to bless the body of Christ—most of God's people are called to obscurity. This is the beauty of the church. Every week congregations around the world gather, filled with ordinary, unspectacular people. Some meet in giant cathedrals, some in storefronts, some in caves under threat of persecution.

God's work in the world is not dependent on any of us going viral. The apostle Paul knew this, which is why he reminded the Corinthians that "not many of you were wise by human standards; not many were influential; not many were of noble birth" (1 Cor. 1:26).

The truth is that to be agents of grace, to be Christians who obey God's call to go into the world and share his love, does not require us to be rich or famous. If you are like me, you often have days when you feel your feeble efforts as a Christian are kind of useless. That kind note you wrote, those tired mornings you spent caring for children, that article you published in your church newsletter all seem like thimblefuls of water in an ocean. And yet this is how the Spirit of God works in the world—not through the mighty or the strong but among the weak and lowly and deeply flawed. Christ is building his church mostly with people who will be unknown to history. The kingdom of God is not a kingdom of great people but moves often among the lowly and unknown and disempowered.

This reality should keep us grounded whether our ministries put us in front of thousands or nobody outside our families knows our names. Fame is fleeting, like the temporary thrill of eating cotton candy or like the blowing of a dandelion in the wind. Eventually those fickle crowds will move on to someone else, to another voice, another talent, another celebrity. We can find rest, instead, in the reality that we are known by the one whose name is above every name (Phil. 2:9).

The Quiet Life with God

I don't know what temptations afflict you today as you read this chapter. Perhaps you wrestle with the desire to be known, whether it's the pull to be an online sensation or the dream of a top position in your career or the longing for people to know your name. Maybe you want to be a preacher whose sermons reach thousands or a Christian singer whose music is downloaded by the masses. Or perhaps you just wish someone would notice the good work you are doing in your family, your church, and your community.

Yet it is in the quiet and unseen that we find intimacy with the one who made us and redeemed us and that we learn how to love. Paul, who had a platform in the early church and whose words we still read today, understood this: "Now about your love for one another we do not need to write to you, for you yourselves have been taught by God to love each other. And in fact, you do love all of God's family throughout Macedonia. Yet we urge you, brothers and sisters, to do so more and more, and to make it your ambition to lead a quiet life: You should mind your own business and work with your hands, just as we told you, so that your daily life may win the respect of outsiders and so that you will not be dependent on anybody" (1 Thess. 4:9–12).

Isn't it interesting that the Bible connects love for each other and the pursuit of fame? It is often resentment and misplaced ambition that cause disunity. Someone got a position we wanted. Someone has a platform we crave. Someone got invited to speak at an event instead of us. This thinking leads to jealousy, to sinful attacks on others, to seeing our fellow Christians as obstacles to our flourishing.

The Bible tells us that our ultimate ambition should

be to "lead a quiet life" and to "mind your own business and work with your hands." Love leads us away from self-promotion toward contentment with our calling and the work we have to do. The quiet life in the Word, in community with other believers, in the spiritual disciplines reminds us of our frailty before God. And it chastens us when we think that the only things that matter are the big, public, bold things we do *for* God, when what matters is what God is doing in us to conform us to the likeness of his Son.

Even those with big audiences and huge platforms should earnestly seek the quiet life, the patient obscurity found in a relationship with the God of the universe. Consider this: even Jesus left the crowds and sought his Father alone in prayer. And so should we.

The quiet life with Jesus pushes us away from an obsession with ourselves in an age that rewards expressive individualism. The quiet life keeps us from taking ourselves too seriously and pushes us to look outward in service to others. The quiet life helps us live in accountability and community.

Resisting unnecessary ambition also helps us to love, rather than resent, our brothers and sisters whose callings place them in the public eye. We are tempted to see public Christians as either infallible heroes who need our constant defending or contemptible villains who need our constant rebuke. I'm saddened by the online comments I read almost every day directed toward well-known Christian leaders and Bible teachers. We often stop seeing those in public as people, as fellow Christians who have their own frailties, insecurities, and struggles.

Healthy Christian community allows us to come together as our real selves, not as airbrushed, professionally managed selves. It allows us to see famous folks not as objects to be stared at but as people God loves.

I once had a conversation with a Christian recording artist. He lives in Nashville and was candid with me about how hard it was for him to attend church. It's hard for him to have community with people who see him only as a famous singer. So he constantly gets hit up for favors and fundraisers and other things. He's grateful for his success and often glad to help, but it's hard for him to find friends who see him as a person and not a product.

I've had the same conversations with public officials. Politicians are often on the receiving end of a lot of anger—some deserved, some misplaced. But to get care for their souls, they need an environment where they are seen as fellow brothers and sisters in Christ, not avatars for everyone's hopes and dreams. This also happens to Christian athletes and CEOs.

Now, it's easy for us to hear this and roll our eyes. "Well, that comes with the territory or the money. I'd love to have that problem." But if we are to love our brothers and sisters in Christ, we should not only seek the quiet life with Jesus but also be willing to help others experience that life as well, especially those for whom that pursuit is harder in an age of celebrity.

Christian love requires us both to resist the urge to seek fame for fame's sake and to resist the shallow and destructive tribalism that puts us in different camps with different teachers. Does this mean we can't have a favorite voice whose ministry helps us walk with Jesus? Of course not. I will unashamedly admit that I'm a fan of pastor Tim Keller. I recommend his books. I quote him frequently and I've had the chance to meet him. I'm partial to radio teacher Chuck Swindoll, whose preaching reached me at a critical time in my life. I can't get enough of John Stott, J. I. Packer, Chuck Colson, and R. C. Sproul. I've had the chance to sit under the preaching of Tony Evans, and I consider him to be perhaps one of the greatest preachers of this era. My knees nearly knocked when I met one of my spiritual heroes, Joni Eareckson Tada. I never met Billy Graham, but I have a picture of his 1971 Chicago crusade on my office wall as a testament to that moment when my father walked forward and changed the trajectory of our family. I've read every biography about the man.

I'm sure, as you are reading this, you can point to a book or a sermon or a radio broadcast that made a significant impact on your walk with Jesus. You might have a favorite politician or scientist or actor or musician who seems to support the things you believe in. I don't believe the Bible is saying that it was wrong for some Corinthians to prefer the preaching of Peter or for some Corinthians to prefer the eloquence of Apollos or for some to prefer the tight legal arguments of Paul. But what these words tell us today is that compared with Christ, all of us—famous or infamous, the platformed or the obscure—are frail, fallen sinners. We best love each other when we recognize each other's gifts but refuse to put others on a pedestal. Flattery and the blind following of human beings, however noble they may be, are not love and only set us up for disappointment. Only Jesus satisfies. Only he is worthy of being the ultimate object of our affections.

The Antidote to Celebrity Culture

I want to end this chapter with a story about two examples of servanthood by Christians in positions of power. One is about the late John Stott. Stott, author of bestselling books such as *The Cross of Christ*, was rector of All Souls Church in London and one of the most influential Christian leaders in the twentieth century. In 2005, *Time* named him one of the hundred most influential people in the world. But Stott lived humbly and used his position to serve the church, including providing resources for Christians in some of the most underserved places around the world.

Theologian and missionary René Padilla once told a story about his experience on a speaking tour with Stott to a remote place in Argentina. To get to their hotel, they had to walk through mud and rain, which obviously soiled their shoes. The next morning Padilla was awakened by a sound outside of his room. When he opened the door, he found perhaps the worlds' most famous theologian, the founder of worldwide ministries, wiping off Padilla's shoes.

This spiritual leader was not above serving in ways that others would probably find demeaning. Padilla said this about John Stott: "Many times I heard him speak about humility. Many more times I saw him live it."[3]

There's another story about an influential journalist in Washington, DC, named Mike Allen. Allen founded two widely read publications, and his newsletters are read every morning by everyone in the nation's capital. *New York Times Magazine* once profiled Allen as "the man the White House wakes up to."[4] Pretty heady stuff. Yet a longtime colleague wrote this about Mike, a committed Christian: "I'll never forget asking Mike Allen, my co-founder and co-author, how he grew kinder as his public prominence— and power—soared. 'I don't understand how you could *not* get more humble. It's obvious how much luck and help it took to get me here,' he said." This colleague then compared Allen to Mr. Rogers and described these uncommon traits that they share:

- Authentic humility
- Intense interest in others
- Unusual optimism
- Minimalist living
- Deep faith[5]

I give these examples to show that there is a way to use our gifts to serve others. Stott resisted the temptation to leverage his notoriety for self-gratification, to live in such an entitled way as to be a reproach to Christ. And Allen, a powerful journalist in Washington, where power is seen as the only currency, selflessly serves others.

Most of us will never find the notoriety of John Stott or Mike Allen. Yet in our small spheres of influence, whether it's a small group, our church, our community, or an online place where we gather, we can leverage our influence either to exalt ourselves or to serve others. Whether we have thousands of online followers or only a handful of friends, whether we have books on the bestseller lists or nobody knows our name, living the "quiet and peaceable" life described in 1 Thessalonians is possible because we follow the one who set the example by using power for the benefit of others. Jesus, before he went to the cross, washed the feet of the disciples, including the one who would betray him, including the one who would deny him, including those who would desert him out of fear.

My wife and I have begun, lately, to describe people like this as "having no guile," the kind of disposition that Australian pastor Mark Sayers describes as a "nonanxious presence."[6]

To be free of the need to perform for an audience, to resist the pull of tribalism, is to be free to live in obedience to an audience of one and leverage our resources and power and gifts on behalf of those God has called us to serve. This humility frees us from the resentments that fuel so many of our petty disputes and allow us to reserve courage to fight for what really matters.

Part 2

Worthy Fights

Chapter 6

The Good Fight

I like to hear a man dwell much on the same essentials of Christianity. . . . It is the essentials and common truths, as I have often said, that we daily live upon as our bread and drink.

—**Richard Baxter,** *The Practical Works of Richard Baxter*

We've seen quite a bit about what the Bible says about unity and fighting over ridiculous things. But, you might ask, don't our beliefs and convictions matter? Surely there are some things worth fighting for, right?

The answer is yes, there are important things worth fighting for. But we need to understand what conflicts are important for Christians and which ones are not. After all, sometimes the Bible urges us to "earnestly contend" and "stand firm," and other times it warns against "foolish arguments" and "empty chatter." And this was before Twitter was invented!

Believe it or not there is a way to think about this. But first, let me offer two examples from recent memory that can provide some context for worthy and unworthy fights. In 2011, a book titled *Love Wins* caused more than a little controversy among evangelical Christians. It seemed to question some things Christians have believed throughout church history, such as the idea that a relationship with God and salvation from sin can be found only through faith in Jesus Christ.[1]

Another controversy happened a few years ago in many churches in the West, particularly in the United States. It involved COVID regulations and what churches should do in terms of restricting access, encouraging vaccinations, and wearing masks. I don't have to remind you how this split families and friends and churches.

Both of these controversies might be over by the time you are reading this book, replaced by new flashpoints. How do we know which things are worth fighting for and which things fall in the category of foolish arguments? This is crucial for Christians to understand. In his book *Evangelical Truth: A Personal Plea for Unity, Integrity, and Faithfulness*, John Stott writes, "We need a greater measure of discernment, so that we may distinguish between evangelical essentials which cannot be compromised and those *adiaphora* (matters indifferent) which, being of secondary importance, it is not necessary for us to follow."[2]

We Actually Do Talk about Fight Club

We've spent a lot of time in this book lamenting division among brothers and sisters in Christ. The Bible is not silent on this, urging Christians to resist sinning against each other with their mouths (James 3). The Bible even says that much of the conflict among church members is the result of a heart problem (James 4:1–4).

Still, the Bible does tell us that there is a time to stand up and fight. Listen to what the apostle Paul tells his protege Timothy, a young pastor of the church of Ephesus: "Fight the good fight of the faith," Paul urges Timothy. "Take hold of the eternal life to which you were called when you made your good confession in the presence of many witnesses" (1 Tim. 6:12). In his last letter, before he was executed by Rome for the crime of preaching the gospel, Paul declares that he has "fought the good fight" (2 Tim. 4:7–8).

Scripture often uses language of conflict, urging us to "put on the full armor of God" (Eph. 6:10–18) and to "be on your guard; stand firm in the faith; be courageous; be strong" (1 Cor. 16:13). Of course, our fight is ultimately against an unseen foe, an enemy the Bible describes as "prowl[ing] around like a roaring lion looking for someone to devour" (1 Peter 5:8). Yet this ultimate spiritual conflict often manifests in conflicts with others.

Jesus told his disciples in the Upper Room—before he was led to the cross to defeat Satan and secure our salvation—that to follow him was often to follow him into trouble. "They hated me," Jesus says, talking about a world without his love, "they will hate you" (John 15:18). This is why there are times to stand up for truth.

It's possible to be deceived by religious teaching that sounds Christian but is false and leads to deception and away from Christ. The Bible mentions this a lot. Here is one example: "But I am afraid that just as Eve was deceived by the serpent's cunning, your minds may somehow be led astray from your sincere and pure devotion to Christ" (2 Cor. 11:3).

So there is a time to fight, to guard against ideas that are spiritually harmful. John Piper says it well: "Right thinking about what the Bible teaches about God and man and salvation really matters. Bad theology dishonors God and hurts people. Churches that sever the root of truth may flourish for a season, but they will wither eventually or turn into something besides a Christian church."[3]

There are things worth fighting for. A body of truth has been passed down from Scripture, through the apostles and prophets, and given to us as a gift. Jesus said to the apostles that he would illuminate them in a special way and reveal his Word to them: "I have much more to say to you, more than you can now bear. But when he, the Spirit of truth, comes, he will guide you into all the truth. He will not speak on his own; he will speak only what he hears, and he will tell you what is yet to come" (John 16:12–13). In Acts 5:32, Peter says that he and the other apostles were "witnesses of these things." This essentially describes the giving of the New Testament. This plus the Old Testament, revealed by Jesus to men like Moses and the prophets, form the basis of God's revealed Word to us (Eph. 2:20), a Word we can trust with our lives (2 Tim. 3:16–17).

The Bible describes this body of truth in different ways, but always as something that must be cherished, preserved, and passed on to the next generation:

- In 1 Timothy 6:20, we are told to "guard what has been entrusted to your care."
- First Timothy 4:6, 11 tells us to "point these things out" and to "command and teach these things."
- First Corinthians 16:13 urges us to "stand firm in the faith."

- In Jude 3, we are told that God's people must "contend earnestly for the faith that was once for all handed down to the saints" (NASB).
- Hebrews 10:23 urges us to "hold fast the profession of our faith without wavering" (KJV).

What are "these things" and "the faith which was once for all handed down to the saints"? What is the Bible talking about when it describes "the profession of our faith"? The Bible here is talking about basic Christian doctrine. Today we sometimes hear well-meaning pastors or leaders say things like "doctrine doesn't matter" or "loving Jesus is more important than doctrine." But doctrines are merely the way we think about God. They are what God has told us about himself and about his Son, Jesus Christ. Studying theology should lead us to worship and awe and wonder. Understanding and appreciating and believing truth about Jesus is part of what it means to love him.

We defend orthodoxy not because we want to be seen as right but because Christian theology is beautiful. It is truth revealed about ourselves, about our world, and, most important, about the God who loves us and about his Son, who died for us.

Imagine saying about a best friend or your spouse or one of your children, "Learning about them doesn't matter as long as I just love them." How absurd, right? To best love my wife, I should learn more things about her, what she likes and dislikes, how she is wired.

Imagine that someone came along and shared with

me things that were flatly untrue about Angela. Imagine I said, "Yeah, I'm not going to fight about those things. All that matters is that I love my wife." Um, that won't work. How loved would Angela feel if I were passe about untruths someone spread about her? Instead, I should be vigilant that everyone I know knows what is true and good and beautiful about the wife I'm sharing my life with.

So you see why the Bible urges us to reject false teaching and fight for truth? We stand up for orthodoxy because this is one way we love the one who saved us from our sin and walks in relationship with us.

The Right Hills to Die On

So how do we know which things in the Bible are worth fighting unwaveringly for and which are issues about which Christians might disagree? This is vitally important not only because we have limited energy, time, resources, and passion but also because we should not want to unnecessarily divide from brothers and sisters in Christ and provoke unneeded conflict.

Christians have been thinking about this for all of church history, but most recently, theologians have labeled this kind of work "theological triage," a term coined by scholar Albert Mohler Jr. He explains it this way:

The word triage comes from the French word trier, which means "to sort." Thus, the triage officer in the medical context is the front-line agent for deciding which patients need the most urgent treatment. Without such a process, the scraped knee would receive the same urgency of consideration as a gunshot wound to the chest. The same discipline that brings order to the hectic arena of the Emergency Room can also offer great assistance to Christians defending truth in the present age.

A discipline of theological triage would require Christians to determine a scale of theological urgency that would correspond to the medical world's framework for medical priority.[4]

I've taken my kids to the emergency room more times than I can count. The best emergency rooms understand how to triage, how to prioritize the most urgent cases from cases that are less urgent, though still important. We need to learn how do this with conflicts among Christians. We don't want to devote our passions to hangnail arguments when spiritual heart surgery needs our attention.

Mohler urges Christians to think of doctrines and beliefs in three categories: first-tier issues, secondary issues, and tertiary issues. In his excellent book *Finding the Right Hills to Die On*, Gavin Ortlund expands this to four categories:

- "First-rank doctrines are *essential* to the gospel.
- "Second-rank doctrines are *urgent* for the church (but not essential to the gospel).
- "Third-rank doctrines are *important* to Christian theology (but not essential to the gospel or necessarily urgent for the church).

- "Fourth-rank doctrines are *indifferent* (they are theologically unimportant)."[5]

Sorting out important doctrines from the less important is not a new practice. The most important creeds in the Christian faith—creeds recited weekly in many church traditions—were hammered out as Christians through the ages tried to put in one document what is important for Christians to believe.

These major Christian creeds are the Apostles' Creed, the Nicene Creed, the Chalcedonian Creed, and the Athanasian Creed. In varying ways, these statements summarize the essentials, the first-tier beliefs of the Christian faith, doctrines such as Jesus' virgin birth, resurrection, and deity. Mohler writes, "The earliest creeds and councils of the church were, in essence, emergency measures taken to protect the central core of Christian doctrine. At historic turning-points such as the councils at Nicaea, Constantinople, and Chalcedon, orthodoxy was vindicated and heresy was condemned—and these councils dealt with doctrines of unquestionable first-order importance."[6]

There are beliefs that are clear from a study of Scripture that were you to deny them, you would put yourself outside of the historic Christian faith. These include important contemporary issues such as the Bible's vision for human sexuality and gender, and the authority and reliability of Scripture. The church has always considered these to be first-tier doctrines.[7] Scholars Donald Fortson and Rollin Grams are right when they say that "one of the primary things handed down in the Christian church over the centuries is a consistent set of ethical instructions, including specific directives about sexual behavior. The church of every generation from the time of the apostles has condemned sexual sin as unbecoming of a disciple of Jesus. At no point have any orthodox Christian teachers ever suggested that one's sexual practices may deviate from biblical standards."[8]

Historians, including many who are not professing Christians, have affirmed this to be true.[9]

And again, we believe this not to be contrarian or to be proven right but because we believe the Creator knows what is best for human flourishing.[10]

I want to pause here to say that there is something beautiful and refreshing and life-giving about knowing that when we step into church and recite a Christian creed or sing a song or hymn with lyrics that articulate precious truths, we join millions of believers from every nation, tribe, and tongue down through history. Studying theology should not be a dry, boring exercise but a pursuit that brings us farther up and further into knowing the one who embodies our beliefs.

Underneath the first-order doctrines are beliefs that are important but secondary. These are issues that Christians have disagreed about for much of church history, such as the nature of baptism. Now, to be sure, while disagreeing on these issues doesn't make someone a less faithful Christian, that doesn't mean the issues aren't important. This is typically the level at which denominations are formed. I'm a Baptist. I believe strongly in what is referred to as "credo-baptism," which is the belief that water baptism by immersion is an ordinance reserved for someone who professes faith in Christ. My Presbyterian brothers and sisters believe differently. They couldn't be members at my church, and I likely couldn't be a member at theirs, and that's okay. I can partner with them on many gospel initiatives because we agree on the first-tier issues.

Then there are third-tier issues, which include topics such as eschatology (beliefs about the end times), the role of sign gifts, the age of the earth, what Bible translation is best to use, and so on. Even Christians in the same church might disagree with one another on these issues. And while I think it is good and right to have strong views on even these tertiary issues, we should be openhanded with others who have differing views. These are ideas about which we may be confident, but not so confident we would be willing to die for them.

Of course, sometimes this division of issues into three or four tiers is complicated. Some issues such as debates over Calvinism or speaking in tongues become important depending on the church tradition. A Presbyterian church likely will not have too many people who don't hold to at least some of the tenets of Reformed theology. An Assemblies of God or Pentecostal church would be a difficult place for someone who doesn't necessarily believe in speaking in tongues. A Methodist church mostly likely would be an uncomfortable place for a Calvinist. At the same time, some fellowships allow for healthy disagreement on such things.

What's important is the way we think about those who differ with us on secondary and tertiary issues. While we might have substantive debates and land in a different place than a brother or sister who thinks differently about, say, the age of the earth or how exactly the end times will unfold or the sign gifts, we should not consider them to be unfaithful or less of a Christian because they have come to a different place on an issue that Christians throughout the ages have historically disagreed about. We should also have grace when we apply our beliefs in public, whether it is the way we choose to educate our children or the way we use our voices in the public square.

I've heard many people lament that Christians disagree on third-tier issues and have throughout the ages. But when I look across the Christian landscape and see faithful believers organizing in various traditions and denominations, I see a mosaic, a beautiful diversity among the people of God. And each tradition and denomination brings an emphasis and perspective that, if we allow it, can shape us in profound ways. My library today is filled with treasures from various church traditions. I'd be impoverished if the only spiritual formation I received came from the denomination in which I'm most comfortable. I'm a proud Baptist and will be all my life. I think our movement has been a blessing to God's people, with our emphasis on evangelism, expository preaching, and the concept of a free church in a free state. Yet I learn from those with whom I disagree and grow as a result.

Picking the things we fight for means we don't all

worship in the same tradition. It also means there are different ways we can partner together, depending on our specific convictions. Biblical unity and picking the right fights sometimes looks like a Baptist church and a Presbyterian church and a Methodist church agreeing on the basics of the gospel and partnering in prayer for their city or on an evangelism initiative. But it also sometimes looks like not partnering in other areas because of strong disagreement on the way we organize our churches. This is okay.

Christian communities don't have to be monolithic. We can have reasoned debates about our disagreements. But we can also save our energy and our fighting spirit to stand firm in those places where we must not budge. All Christians share a precious body of truth handed down to us from the apostles, kept alive by the Spirit in two thousand years of church history, which shapes the life of Christ among his people.

Fighting for Purity

Another fight worth having is the fight for the witness and purity of the church. In his first letter to the Corinthians, Paul rebukes and pleads with them to address the rampant sexual sin among the church's members:

> It is actually reported that there is sexual immorality among you, and of a kind that even pagans do not tolerate: A man is sleeping with his father's wife. And you

are proud! Shouldn't you rather have gone into mourning and have put out of your fellowship the man who has been doing this? For my part, even though I am not physically present, I am with you in spirit. As one who is present with you in this way, I have already passed judgment in the name of our Lord Jesus on the one who has been doing this. So when you are assembled and I am with you in spirit, and the power of our Lord Jesus is present, hand this man over to Satan for the destruction of the flesh, so that his spirit may be saved on the day of the Lord.

Your boasting is not good. Don't you know that a little yeast leavens the whole batch of dough? Get rid of the old yeast, so that you may be a new unleavened batch—as you really are. For Christ, our Passover lamb, has been sacrificed. Therefore let us keep the Festival, not with the old bread leavened with malice and wickedness, but with the unleavened bread of sincerity and truth.

—1 Corinthians 5:1–8

This church was in a sensual city, and rather than demonstrating to their community the power of the gospel to change lives, rather than pointing to a more flourishing sexual ethic in a culture that boasted of sexual license, these Christians were boastful about the habitual sins they permitted in their midst.

Today our churches are located in cultures not much different than Corinth. Churches should be filled with redeemed sinners, people whose lives are checkered up and down and yet have been forgiven by Jesus. But if we are not careful, we will adopt the cheap grace of Corinth that forgets that the gospel calls us away from the idolatries and habits of the age. Rather than calling their members up toward holiness, the Corinthians excused rampant, unrepentant sin. Rather than reveling in the love and grace of God, they used the cross of Christ as an excuse to continue to pursue ungodly lifestyles. No believer is perfect. Every member of a church, even those who have been faithfully walking with Jesus for decades, is a sinner in need of God's grace and grace from fellow believers. And yet continued, habitual, unrepentant sin dishonors Christ. And a church that allows this to persist fails to show the world what the alternate community of God's people looks like.

Sometimes, for the sake of unity, Christians are tempted to overlook gross sin or abuse by their leaders, such as sexual abuse or financial improprieties or an abusive temper. But leaders should be held accountable.

The witness of the church is a fight worth having, even if these confrontations should be conducted with sensitivity and humility. Jesus outlines a process for conflicts such as these in Matthew 18, which involves first personal then public accountability and a plan for restoration. Sometimes problems rise to the level of church discipline that Paul outlines in 1 Corinthians 5. But even this step of last resort should be taken only for the health of the church and the spiritual health of the unrepentant member. And it should be taken with humility and discretion. Too often fights play out publicly, on social media, in major media outlets, with leaked letters and recorded phone calls. In some circumstances, such as criminal behavior, this is necessary and unavoidable, but it's far more important that God's people handle conflicts with wisdom, discretion, and care. It's disunifying to tolerate sin. In some cases, especially in the case of sexual abuse, the church should turn to civil authorities.

It's not unloving or disunifying to address unrepentant immorality in the life of a church member. It's the most loving thing a faithful body of believers can do. Galatians tells us that God uses the Christian community to help restore someone from sin: "Brothers and sisters, if someone is caught in a sin, you who live by the Spirit should restore that person gently. But watch yourselves, or you also may be tempted" (Gal. 6:1).

How We Fight

Even as we engage in battles worth fighting, as we obey the Word of God and stand up, with courage, for the truth of the gospel, even as we nourish ourselves with the rich treasure of historic Christian teaching, we should also heed what the Bible says about the way we fight.

Immediately after the passage in 1 Corinthians 16, which urges us to stand firm in the faith, we are also told to "do everything in love" (v. 14). Peter, urging the first-century church on toward courage, says to "always be prepared to give an answer to everyone who asks you to give the reason for the hope that you have. But do this with gentleness and respect" (1 Peter 3:15).

The Bible cares about how we fight. We should not shrink from important conflicts about the truth, but we should approach every conflict with humility: "Do nothing out of selfish ambition or vain conceit. Rather, in humility value others above yourselves, not looking to your own interests but each of you to the interests of the others" (Phil. 2:3–4).

If we stand up for doctrine but fail to demonstrate the fruit of the Spirit, we deny the very doctrine we claim to be defending. If our pastors and ministry leaders write and speak about important spiritual truths but are quarrelsome, lack grace, and don't give others the benefit of the doubt, they fail to meet the temperamental qualifications for Christian leadership (1 Timothy 3; Titus 1). Paul urges leaders to exemplify reasonableness and kindness, traits every believer should cultivate with the help of the Spirit. We should care about these virtues whether or not we serve in a leadership position. Every Christian is being observed by others.

Sometimes I hear Christians justify harsh language and demeaning vitriol by pointing to Jesus' turning over the tables in the temple. But we should remember that we are not Jesus, given a divine mandate by the Father to cleanse and purify God's house. And while we know Jesus' motives when angry were always justified, we can't be as sure about our own. Jesus is also the one who is known for being "full of grace and truth" (John 1:14). He is the one who is "gentle and humble in heart" (Matt. 11:29). We should work to embody these traits as well. This means we offer other Christians the benefit of the doubt (1 Corinthians 13), avoid making accusations, and don't treat lesser doctrines as primary. The fruit of the Spirit (Gal. 5:22–23) is not conditional based on the moment.

Which brings us back to the examples we discussed at the beginning of this chapter. Some Christians' attempt to deny the existence of hell or to embrace universalist beliefs that allow for all people to spend eternity with God without confession of sin and faith in Christ is a departure from Christian orthodoxy. This is a movement away from the Bible's clear teaching on Christ as the way to salvation, and that clear teaching is worth fighting for. Conversely, the battle over how best to handle COVID, a debate that so divided churches, falls into the category of things good and faithful Christians can disagree on. And our squabbles over how best to articulate our beliefs among people who generally agree distracts us from fighting for and proclaiming with confidence the beautiful truths of the Christian faith.

It doesn't matter only *that* we fight but also *how* we fight and *what* we fight about. It strikes me that in recent years, most of the time Christians are fighting over issues that don't rise to the level of primary or even secondary issues. There is a fierce battle in every generation to uphold faithful Christian orthodoxy, and ours is no different. And we should be known as joyful warriors who embrace the beauty and wonder of God's revealed truth.

We should resist the urge to fight over dumb things, over tertiary things, to split over issues not worth dividing over. Which brings us, with some trepidation, to that field where church members seem to generate the most conflict: politics.

Chapter 7

Religion and Politics

Never succumb to the temptation of becoming bitter. As you press for justice, be sure to move with dignity and discipline, using only the instruments of love.

—**Martin Luther King Jr.,** "The Most Durable Power"

I want to start this chapter with a story about two steak dinners. I'm not a betting man, but I had an agreement with my brother-in-law that began sometime in 2015, after Donald Trump came down that gold escalator at Trump Tower and announced he was running for president. I was convinced Trump wouldn't win. My brother-in-law, who was a Trump supporter from that first announcement, was convinced he would. You must keep in mind that I've been in and around politics my entire life. I've helped friends win races. I've consulted public officials. I've been voraciously reading about politics since I was a nerdy kid in high school reading *National Review*. In my leisure time I read presidential biographies, and if I'm ever within two hours' driving distance of a presidential library, I go. I once made my son spend half a day at the James K. Polk home in obscure Columbia, Tennessee, because his summer camp was thirty minutes away and to miss the place where our eleventh president lived just seemed wrong.

So I dismissed my brother-in-law (and millions of others, apparently). I was so confident Trump wouldn't win the Republican primary, I told Randy that if he did, I'd owe him a steak dinner.

Well, let's just say that by early summer 2016, my wallet was a little lighter and my stomach a little heavier.

But because I hadn't yet learned my lesson, I predicted that there was no way Donald Trump would beat Hillary Clinton. He was behind in the polls. He lacked support from the establishment of his own party. And while he ran with a slogan that promised to "make America great again," his public appearances demonstrated that he was a walking insult and gaffe machine. Winning candidates, I told my brother-in-law, just don't do these things. Trust me, I said. And again, I promised a steak dinner if the election in November went for Donald Trump.

Well, you know how this worked out. I ended up having to buy my victorious and not-at-all-humble-about-it brother-in-law yet another steak dinner.

I've got to be honest. Though I've been a conservative my entire life, active in politics, writing and advocating for conservative policy positions, I couldn't bring myself to support Trump because of his character and unprofessional behavior. So for the first time in my life, I voted third party. (As a sidenote, the tweets of the third-party guy I voted for became insufferable and I stopped following him on social media. Ugh, the despair of 2016!)

But I learned something in that election cycle and in the years since. Not only did I miss an entire group of people for whom Donald Trump spoke, I realized how visceral politics can be and how it has increasingly become a divisive force in our families, churches, and communities.

Thankfully, my brother-in-law and I enjoy a wonderful relationship. I've come around to seeing some of the reasons he pulled the lever for our forty-fifth president, and he has come around to seeing some of the reservations I had about him. And when Donald Trump was president, I tried my best both to pray for him and to fairly evaluate his decisions, as I've tried to do with every president in my lifetime. I could share similar stories about friendships I have with progressive-leaning friends.

But I'm realizing that my experience is somewhat unique as politics has become a bloodsport, rending asunder once-solid friendships, dividing parents and children, and becoming for too many of us a replacement religion.

Why Politics Matters

Because our politics is so exhausting, many pastors and Christians wonder whether we should even get engaged in the messy business at all. The thinking goes like this: politics just makes people mad at each other, and when Christians get involved, it hurts the work of Jesus. I sympathize with this sentiment quite a bit. As a pastor, as a denominational leader, as a professor in a Christian institution, I see up close the wreckage politics makes of non-Christians' perception of the church.

And yet I wonder whether we can avoid engaging our world. Jesus told us that the greatest commandment in all of Scripture is to love God with all our hearts and to love our neighbors as ourselves. In a representative democracy like we have in the United States and in the other democracies around the world, I wonder whether we Christians can claim to love our neighbors if we don't participate with our voices and our votes in shaping the social structures that our neighbors inhabit. Can I really say that I'm loving my unborn neighbor as myself if, when given a chance, I say nothing or do nothing when their lives are threatened? Can I say to my minority neighbors that I'm loving them as myself if I don't speak up about injustice? Can I say to my neighbors with struggling families that I love them as myself if I don't speak up against economic and social policies that threaten their flourishing? I don't think we can simply wash our hands and say, "I don't do politics."

The impulse is well meaning, of course. We often are so defined by our politics, whether we consistently vote Republican or vote Democratic. Yet to withdraw—whatever that looks like—is not as simple of a solution as we might think. There are times when to say nothing or do nothing is itself a political statement.

Consider the way many Christians resisted saying anything, for instance, about segregation and Jim Crow laws in the Deep South in the twentieth century. Saying nothing, not rocking the boat, baptized the status quo and allowed systemic racism to flourish. This point was the essence of Martin Luther King Jr.'s "Letter from Birmingham Jail." Or consider pastors today whose preaching calendar includes Psalm 139 ("You created my inmost being; you knit me together in my mother's womb," v. 13) and are hesitant to apply that to the issue of abortion. By saying nothing, do they sanction evil?

The truth is, we who were born in this country are stewards of a citizenship that makes us accountable to God for the influence we possess. In Romans 13, we are given instructions on how Christians should relate to our governments. Most Christians have read this passage and understand it to mean we should obey those who ultimately are put in power by God unless it causes us to violate Scripture. And yet I think there are deeper implications here:

> Let everyone be subject to the governing authorities, for there is no authority except that which God has established. The authorities that exist have been established by God. Consequently, whoever rebels against the authority is rebelling against what God has instituted, and those who do so will bring judgment on themselves. For rulers hold no terror for those who do right, but for those who do wrong. Do you want to be free from fear of the one in authority? Then do what is right and you will be commended. For the one in authority is God's servant for your good. But if you do wrong, be afraid, for rulers do not bear the sword for no reason. They are God's servants, agents of wrath to bring punishment on the wrongdoer. Therefore, it is necessary to submit to the authorities, not only because of possible punishment but also as a matter of conscience.
>
> This is also why you pay taxes, for the authorities are God's servants, who give their full time to governing. Give to everyone what you owe them: If you owe taxes, pay taxes; if revenue, then revenue; if respect, then respect; if honor, then honor.
>
> **—Romans 13:1–7**

Let's do a thought experiment. The people to whom Paul was writing were a persecuted minority living under a cruel and capricious dictator, Nero. They had little, if any, recourse to change their government. Concepts like private property, personal liberty, and freedom of conscience were centuries away from being realized in any society. Paul's words to the Christians in Rome were a comfort, telling them that despite what it looked like, despite the nearly four-century campaign of terror against Christians that would ensue, God was in control and earthly rulers ruled only at his discretion. So to honor Christ was to pay their taxes, to be good citizens when they could, and to trust in God's sovereignty.

Those lessons apply to us today. They are healthy reminders that we shouldn't sweat the headlines or clutch our pearls every time an election doesn't go our way. Yet buried in here is a statement about our responsibility in a country where power is decentralized. Here power is shared equally among three branches of government, a nod to the founders' recognition of human depravity and the danger of absolute control by one person or entity.

Furthermore, the US Constitution decentralizes power even more. Consider the first line of the preamble, which opens like this: "We the people, in order to form a more perfect union." Abraham Lincoln, perhaps our greatest president, summarized the American creed as a government "of the people, by the people, and for the people."

Of course, an argument can be made that in some chapters of our history, some entities have held too much power, such as white slave owners during antebellum slavery or the executive branch in the modern era or perhaps the Supreme Court at certain moments in our history. Those political statements, though, point to the central design of our system, which is supposed to empower ordinary people to shape their government.

Why this civics lesson? Applying Romans 13 to our system of government means that it's not merely those who hold elected or appointed office who should understand why God allowed them to rule. We ordinary people possess power, however little, to shape our society. We don't have the option to withdraw, because in many ways, *we* are the government Romans 13 is talking about. We are "God's servant for your good" (v. 4) in the world we inhabit.

We might also consider that to be a follower of Jesus is to be political. Not partisan, not tribal, but political. Assembling every week at church to declare that there is another king and another kingdom is a political statement. The crux of our faith is a rebuke to the idolatries of the age. When first-century Christians in the Roman Empire refused to bow down and worship Caesar, and declared that an itinerant Jewish rabbi from Nazareth was the King of Kings and was coming back again in triumph over the nations, they were making a profoundly political statement.

If you believe that the Bible teaches us something about certain matters, such as about the evil of racism or the moral horror of abortion, you are political. If you believe the Bible teaches us something about sexual ethics or the goodness of humans being created male and female, you are political. If you believe the Bible teaches us something about stealing someone else's private property or bearing false witness, then you are political. That following Jesus will put you, at times, at odds with the prevailing culture doesn't mean you are doing something wrong. There are times when "friendship with the world means enmity against God" (James 4:4). It's also true that being at odds with the culture doesn't always mean that you are being faithful to Christ. Christianity isn't always contrarian. Sometimes people don't like us because we are unlikable.

The question before us, then, is not whether to engage the political systems of the country into which we have been born and where we continue to live but *how* to engage them. This is where, as followers of Jesus, we must be different from our neighbors.

We Need a Better Politics

If we can't escape it, how do we do politics in a redemptive way? How do we avoid letting the important and necessary work of loving our neighbors keep us from building walls and dividing Christians unnecessarily?

First, we should put politics in its place. Having a say in who holds office and influencing what policies they enact is important, but it's not our ultimate concern. We should not do politics in a way that makes it the most important thing we care about. I say this because this is my temptation.

C. S. Lewis had a word about the way we order things. We can take something really good, like politics, and give it a focus we should give only to our love for God: "There is but one good; that is God. Everything else is good when it looks to him and bad when it turns from him. And the higher and mightier it is in the natural order, the more demoniac it will be if it rebels. It's not out of bad mice or bad fleas you make demons, but out of bad archangels. The false religion of lust is baser than the false religion of mother-love or patriotism or art: but lust is less likely to be made into a religion."[1]

Politics can become all-consuming, possessive, formative. It can color the way we look at people around us, the lens by which we see everything. I think one of the reasons our communities are often so divided is because we've replaced religious fervor with political fervor.

As followers of Jesus, we must prioritize the kingdom of God. We may belong to a political party, we may vote a certain way, we may advocate for certain issues, but ultimately, we are Jesus' people.

The book of James gives us some wisdom here: "Religion that God our Father accepts as pure and faultless is this: to look after orphans and widows in their distress and to keep oneself from being polluted by the world" (1:27).

Notice the inside-outside approach? We must care and advocate for the vulnerable while also tending to the state of our souls. The spiritual disciplines of prayer and Scripture reading and community with our fellow believers are vital, especially in an age when so many things vie for our attention and affection. Staying close to Jesus reminds us of the temporal nature of our politics. Every earthly government, even in a country as wonderful as ours, will one day fade away. But Christ's kingdom is eternal.

It's also important when we are doing politics to ask ourselves *why* we are doing politics. Why are we posting that thing on Twitter or Facebook? Are we truly speaking up on a particular issue or are we just broadcasting that we are not like people in some other group? Are we acting on behalf of our neighbors, or is our activism a vehicle to vent our rage or to let the world know that we belong to the right group?

Pastor Scott Sauls offers a helpful warning:

> While rising up to advance righteousness, God's people must also engage the inner battle to "sin not" in their anger (Ps. 4:4; Eph. 4:26). On the one hand, anger can serve as an instrument of true peace. Such righteous anger can be necessary and constructive. Many of the world's most important human-rights initiatives— abolishing the slave trade, confronting sex trafficking, initiating the #MeToo and #ChurchToo movements that expose abuse of power, opposing Hitler, advancing civil rights and more—have harnessed the energy of righteous anger. These movements began because a person or group of people went public with their collective, righteous anger. On the other hand, if we are not careful, anger that starts out as righteous can become unrighteous, injurious, and counter-productive to the name and cause of Jesus Christ.[2]

Anger can be a useful vehicle against injustice, but we often assume that, in politics, the shrillest person is doing the most good. But frankly, in my advocacy work in Washington, DC, and in state capitals around the country, I've found that the most effective agents of change are often people who are the least likely to say something provocative. We might equate action with angry tweets or Facebook posts, but while those efforts are often effective at gathering an audience, they are less effective at galvanizing a coalition to change the law.

Our involvement in politics might also change depending on our callings. God raises up some to run for office, to write and speak, to be advocates. But others are called to quieter work in communities around the country, in ways that aren't so obviously political. That doesn't mean the Christian who runs for office is too political, nor does it mean the Christian who doesn't is a coward. God gifts people in the church differently for different purposes.

We often allow politics to divide us from our brothers and sisters in Christ. In the last few years, I've seen friends who agree on most everything destroy their friendships because they disagree on the proper approach to politics or on who to support for public office. I find it disheartening that people who will share heaven for eternity won't share a pew because they disagree politically.

Part of what it means to love as Jesus commanded us to love in John 17 and as the apostle John exhorted us to love in 1 John is to give others the benefit of the doubt when it comes to politics. God places different passions in his people's hearts. I have friends who have spent their entire lives in relief and development work. Their Christianity has put them in a place of public advocacy for the poor. I have other friends who have spent their entire lives working to combat abortion in America. Their Christianity has put them in a place of public advocacy for the unborn.

It would be tempting for me to see the friend who works for a relief agency as insufficiently active on pro-life issues, but her calling to alleviate poverty has her full focus. It would be similarly tempting for me to see my pro-life activist friend as insufficiently concerned about poverty because her full focus is on the unborn. But the body of Christ needs both advocates.

Don't Divide over Politics

My first political campaign was for my conservative congressman, Phil Crane, who represented my suburban Chicago district when I was a kid. He was a member of my church. I have handed out fliers, knocked on doors, and marched in parades for quite a few candidates. I still have a "Phil Crane '80" button in my home office, a tribute to his quixotic run for president.

As much as we might care about politics, we should never let it destroy our friendships or supersede our love for Christ. Unfortunately, I know folks who agree theologically on almost every single issue and yet won't speak to each other because they were on opposite sides of an election.

What encourages me is that in the midst of so much division in our country, we often see rare glimpses of Christian love in politics. One of my favorite stories is of Cal Thomas and Bob Beckel. Cal is a longtime conservative columnist, a one-time architect of the Moral Majority. To say Cal is a conservative is an understatement. Bob was a liberal who worked for Al Gore and was on the opposite political side from Cal Thomas. But both worked, at one time, as analysts on Fox News. Bob recently passed away and this is what Cal wrote about him:

> We traveled together, ate together, and got to know each other and our respective "stories" in ways that rarely happen in Washington these days. At the end of our presentation, I would say that I rejected the notion that Bob was on "the other side." Both of our fathers were in World War II. They weren't fighting for or against Franklin Roosevelt, but to preserve an ideal. America has always been an idea in search of the ideal. If we want to put someone on the other side, make them external enemies like the Ayatollah in Iran, or the leadership in China and Russia. Let's not destroy each other. We are fellow Americans.
>
> Bob would then get up and say how I had saved his life and introduced him to God and other nice things. We embraced, prompting wild cheers from the audience. People would say, "Why can't we see more of this in Washington?" It helped that neither of us were interested in running for office, which would mean having

to raise money and say things to satisfy various interest groups.

At his memorial service this week there will be Republicans and Democrats, liberals and conservatives. It will be a moment of common ground. Bob was my closest and dearest friend. His hope and mine is that our friendship will serve as an example to others of what can be and must be if we are to survive as a nation.[3]

Of course, if you are reading this, you probably aren't thinking about being a political activist or a cable news commentator, but you have people in your life, no doubt, that you find hard to get along with because of their political views. Perhaps you have a son or daughter who seems to get their views on justice from TikTok or a parent who watches too much cable news or listens to too much talk radio. Perhaps you are frustrated because you've seen friends on all sides radicalized by their favorite pundits. Can we find a way to love them?

Love begins by seeing those who disagree with us not as the sum and the substance of that political opinion they hold, the one we think is wrong, the one with which we disagree. Instead, it begins by seeing our brothers and sisters in Christ as fellow heirs of God's grace.

I've not always been good with this, as you can tell from my foolish wagers over dinner and my nearly broken friendship with a lifelong friend. But in the last few years, the Lord has helped me develop friendships across the political divide.

One of my dear friends worked in the Obama administration. As a conservative, I disagree with him on several policy issues, but I have learned a lot from his wisdom and have admired his devotion to Christ, to his marriage, and to his family.

I have another dear friend who worked in the Trump administration. I strongly disagreed with much of Donald Trump's public rhetoric, his reckless personal lifestyle, and his actions after the 2020 election. Yet I admire what my friend was able to accomplish in very difficult circumstances, serving her country.

When I see my progressive friend or my conservative friend, I don't see them merely as extensions of their politics, as if that's all they are. Each is so much more than that.

Politics Shouldn't Make Us Mean

At the end of the day, getting involved, at whatever level we are called to engage, is a matter of stewardship. Some of us need more politics in our lives; we are silent when we should be vocal. But many of us probably could use a bit less. Perhaps it's not healthy to follow the ups and downs of every single news story, the idle political chatter that wastes so much time, the daily intake of opinion that can eat away at our souls. Perhaps it's time to do an audit. Are we so consumed by politics that it is affecting our relationships?

I recently had a conversation with a friend who lamented that while she shared her husband's politics, his daily intake of podcasts and cable news was "making him mean." I wonder how often that can be said of us. I wonder whether in our social media profiles, in our daily conversations, in the things that irritate us we forget that our first job as followers of Jesus is to share the good news of what he has done for us.

This isn't an admonition toward passivity. We need believers to go into the world and make a difference. But we go as God's people, as ambassadors of another kingdom. Even the way we speak, the way we treat people, should reflect the love of Christ.

One of the biggest temptations of politics is being convinced that because our cause is just, we can bypass being formed by the Spirit. In our zeal to gain power and influence, we can lose our Christianity. David French offers a sober warning: "To be sure, some of the best people in public life proclaim the name of Christ. But so do some of the worst. While some of the most important fights for justice have been led by Christians—including the civil rights and pro-life movements—some of the most destructive political and cultural forces have been loudly and proudly led by Christians as well."[4]

Virtues matter. The fruit of the Spirit—love, joy, peace, forbearance, kindness, goodness, faithfulness, gentleness, self-control—doesn't go away merely because our cause is just. God cares about our character as much as he cares about the cause.

Politics—held loosely, approached humbly—can be a wonderful vehicle for meaningful change and human flourishing. But it can also be an arena of temptation, leading us away from Jesus. In recent years, as the stakes have ratcheted up, politics has seeped into the church, distracting us from our mission and turning brothers and sisters against one another.

There is a whole genre of books and articles and other content written by Christians excoriating other Christians for voting differently from them. And while we need prophetic voices, we have so totalized our politics that we ascribe the worst motives and malice to those who punch the ballot differently.

This is a politics that makes us mean. And somewhere along the line, we forget the causes that got us into activism in the first place. Instead of standing up for the vulnerable, instead of working on making change, instead of getting meaningful legislation across the finishing line, our engagement is merely a way to show the world that we are better, more righteous, and nobler than the people we are trying to crush. Too often those we want to destroy are our own brothers and sisters in the Lord, whom we are called to love, whose burdens we are tasked with bearing.

The task of a Christian in the world is to speak up for truth and justice, to work to shape communities for human flourishing, but to do these things in a distinctly Christian way. We can do this when we remember that the battles we are fighting are really spiritual battles. Scripture reminds us, "For our struggle is not against flesh and blood, but against the rulers, against the authorities, against the powers of this dark world and against the spiritual forces of evil in the heavenly realms" (Eph. 6:12).

This is why prayer and other spiritual disciplines are so important for our engagement in politics. We should remember Paul's words to Timothy, a pastor leading a church during the Roman Empire's increasing hostility toward Christians. He told Timothy, "I urge, then, first of all, that petitions, prayers, intercession and thanksgiving be made for all people—for kings and all those in authority, that we may live peaceful and quiet lives in all godliness and holiness. This is good, and pleases God our Savior, who wants all people to be saved and to come to a knowledge of the truth" (1 Tim. 2:1–4).

If the church at Ephesus could pray earnestly for Nero, who would one day send Christians to their deaths for bearing the name of Christ, we can pray for our leaders. It's funny how controversial this idea has become in recent years. For the last several years, I've made it a habit, after every election day, to post prayers for the newly elected president, and it always seems to upset Christian friends who find themselves on the losing side.

So when George W. Bush was elected, I called people to pray, and progressive friends pushed back. When Barack Obama was elected, I did the same thing and got the same flak from conservative friends. And this cycle was repeated when Donald Trump and then Joe Biden were elected. Who knew biblical prayer for our leaders would make folks mad? It shows, I think, how personal we've made our politics, how we've turned genuine political differences into a license to hate. To give an inch, even in prayer, is seen as compromise. To be civil to those who disagree, without budging on our principles, is seen as being complicit with evil.

We have come to this moment not because we care too much about the issues we are championing but because we've elevated the temporal good of politics above faith in our eternal, sovereign, powerful God. If our only hope is in the next election, then we will wring our hands in fear, we'll abandon biblical virtues and the fruit of the Spirit, and we will engage the world with the rhetoric and methods of the world. But if we truly believe that Christ is king and he's coming one day to establish his eternal kingdom, we can engage with both conviction and civility, with both lament over evil and joy in our hearts, with both opposition to bad policies and love for people.

It's possible to do this if we keep ourselves anchored in the Word, in prayer, in faithful Christian community. It will mean that, at times, our Christian convictions will put us at odds with our political parties or movements. But that's okay, because as strangers and sojourners (1 Peter 2:11), we understand that the present world systems, even the best ones in the best countries, are not our final destination.

My friend Michael Wear says it best: "Christians: The crisis is not that you are politically homeless. The crisis is that we ever thought we could make a home in politics at all."[5]

Engaging politics joyfully allows us not only to win others over with persuasive arguments and to stand up for the vulnerable but also to fulfill our calling as witnesses to another kingdom. Our politics should be otherworldly, pointing souls who are seeking to the only true source of satisfaction, Jesus Christ. This is how we function as agents of grace, how we become people eager to be part of God's work of reconciliation in the world.

Chapter 8

Nation, Tribe, Tongue

*The local church should reflect the truth
about God. If it is divided, it teaches
everyone that Christ is divided. If love
does not mark your church, then it may
attract spiritual hobbyists who like to play
at religion, but not people of real Christian
love who will inconvenience themselves for
others.*

—Mark Dever

Exhausted. That's the

sentiment I've heard from pastors across the country since 2020. I don't think there is an issue that has divided Christians more than the issue of race. Good people, who love Jesus, grew bitterly opposed to each other not because they disagree on the problem of racism but because they share different proposals and prescriptions for how to move forward.

These fault lines, to be sure, didn't appear suddenly. They've been there, under the surface, for as long as America has existed—and if you believe the Bible, since the garden of Eden. The ugliness of slavery and Jim Crow laws in our country has a ripple effect that hasn't gone away. Ongoing instability and new racial flashpoints have only reinforced the fraught nature of conversations about race. Many wonder, on all sides, whether racial reconciliation is still possible. This chapter isn't all I have to say on racial unity. I've written on this topic extensively elsewhere.[1] Yet I think that if we are to become agents of grace, it's important to briefly make the case that the project of reconciliation is an important one for the church as well. If we are to build bridges across divides, then we must make racial reconciliation a priority.

Reconciliation Still Matters

Growing up in the mostly white suburbs of Chicago, I was ignorant of issues around race. Of course, we learned about slavery and Jim Crow laws and the civil rights movement, but we weren't immersed in the conversation. My parents abhorred racism and taught us to abhor it, but because we operated mostly in a majority-culture environment, we didn't talk about it much. The only proximity I had to the concerns of a minority were conversations with my few black friends and in conversations with my mother's side of the family. My grandparents, first-generation children of immigrants who fled the pogroms in Europe at the turn of the twentieth century, sometimes spoke of what it was like to be Jewish in America. We read about racial flashpoints in the news, such as the Rodney King riots and Jesse Jackson's run for president. Still, the topic of race just wasn't front and center. We lived in a world not yet connected by the internet, which can rocket news stories around the world and make them major events.

It wasn't until I read *Soul Survivor* by Phillip Yancey that my vision expanded. Yancey wrote about his difficult upbringing in the Deep South in an evangelical church that hosted the KKK and fought bitterly against desegregation. I was shocked by the severity of Jim Crow laws and by too many Christians' complicity in the subhuman treatment of image bearers of God based on the color of their skin. I began to read more about Martin Luther King

Jr. and about the terror of lynching, chronicled so rawly and accurately by Bryan Stevenson in his book *Just Mercy*, and about the systemic injustice of practices like redlining in Isabel Wilkerson's *The Warmth of Other Suns*.

I guess what awakened in me was the recognition that America's original sin of racism is not just a past transgression that has no bearing on the present and the future but something that we have to reckon with today, even as we acknowledge that our country has made extraordinary progress in living up to the high ideal of "all men are created equal." Though I didn't vote for him, because of his liberal social policies, I did cry the night Barack Obama ascended the stage in Grant Park, Illinois, to declare victory as America's first black president. He would live in a house, at 1600 Pennsylvania Avenue, that was built by black slaves, and govern from an office that once banned people who looked like him from even entering. In my conversations with brothers and sisters of color, I've come to understand how their experiences differ from my own as a white man in a majority white country.

As a pastor and denominational leader, I've seen the fraught nature of our discussions about race. I'm proudly Southern Baptist, a denomination made up of fourteen million people. But unfortunately, our history is weaved ignominiously with America's racial history, born as we are of a desire to protect white slave-owners in the 1800s. And yet we've made significant progress in recent years, working hard to reckon with our past, apologizing in a landmark 1995 resolution.[2] We've since released multiple resolutions on racial reconciliation, many in response to racial flashpoints. We've conducted studies and launched projects for kingdom diversity, and we are seeing our greatest growth among multiethnic and minority churches.[3] Still, we have miles to go, riven as we still seem to be by contemporary discussions about race.

Ours is the biggest fellowship of Protestant churches in the US, but in my conversations with leaders in other fellowships, I'm finding similar tensions threatening to divide good people and good work.

Many evangelicals want to throw in the towel. Beat up as they are, by all sides, for attempting to bring brothers and sisters together in love, they wonder whether the fight is worth it. And yet, bearing my own scars, I believe it is.

I do believe we have to approach the topic of race not first as partisans but as the people of God. Both the idea of ethnic reconciliation and the sin of partiality and prejudice existed well before our moment. They were addressed in Scripture centuries before the horrors of chattel slavery, Jim Crow, and systemic racism. Those of us who profess faith in Jesus Christ are bound to listen to what God is saying to us and can believe that he has the answers for what ails our churches, our communities, and our world.

The Bible tells us that sin—from that fateful day in the garden when the human race abandoned their creator—is the root of prejudice, ethnic partiality, and humans' turning on one another. The tendency to see others as less than human is as old as the earth. The Bible calls this what it is: sin against a holy God. Listen to the words of James to the first-century church: "My brothers and sisters, believers in our glorious Lord Jesus Christ must not show favoritism" (James 2:1). This is the same sin that Paul called out because Peter and Barnabas and other Jewish believers refused to accept their gentile brothers and sisters (Galatians 2). Paul called it out because partiality, prejudice, and racism go against God's love for his image bearers and his desire to call out a people from every nation, tribe, and tongue. Way back in Genesis, God promised Abraham that he would be the "father of many nations," or many ethnic groups (Gen. 17:5). Pastor Derwin Gray, in his book *How to Heal Our Racial Divide*, says, "God has always promised a multicolored, multiethnic family to Abraham, and that family was given to him in Jesus Christ. . . . Jesus kept his Father's promise to Abraham through his life, death, and resurrection and through his victory over sin, death, and the powers of darkness. You are a product of the promise-keeping God, and so are your ethnically diverse siblings. Love and unity across ethnic lines were secured at the cross of Christ."[4]

So in a sense, working for ethnic unity in the church is working up into what we already are. Just as Christians we are called every day to "work out [our] salvation in fear and trembling" (Phil. 2:12) even though we are declared righteous by God, so too we should work toward living out the unity we already have as a result of Christ's finished work. Listen to the way the apostle John describes the people of God in the new heaven and new earth: "After this I looked, and there before me was a great multitude that no one could count, from every nation, tribe, people and language, standing before the throne and before the Lamb. They were wearing white robes and were holding palm branches in their hands" (Rev. 7:9).

What a glorious picture! This is the promise of a people gathered by God that was given to Abraham long ago. Today, as much as we work toward ethnic unity in the church, we show the world a glimpse of that beautiful, unified world to come. Gray writes, "God has always longed to have a single, worldwide, multinational, multiethnic family of coheirs and equals in Christ who love him by loving each other. At the heart of ethnic reconciliation is God's heart for the reconciliation of people and creation."[5]

Two Wrong but Well-Meaning Approaches

While many well-meaning Christians seek to be part of the solution to the racial tensions in our day, it seems we are tempted to seek two equally misguided approaches, and this is where much of the current conflict seems to be centered, often fomented by pundits and partisans who profit from division. If we really want God's people to become a picture of the grand unity we will see at the end of the age, if we want the church to be a solution to the issues of race in our society, then we need to anchor our approaches not in worldly models but in biblical approaches.

Jarvis Williams, a scholar at my alma mater, Southern Baptist Theological Seminary, and author of *Redemptive Kingdom Diversity*, warns:

All political and secular models by themselves lead to a dead end, not to a sustained redemptive opposition to racism, because they offer no eternal hope of redemption rooted in the image of God, God's redemptive vision for kingdom diversity through Jesus's death and resurrection, and the indwelling presence and power of the Spirit in God's people. Redemptive kingdom diversity occurs when the people of God pray for and in the power of the Spirit work toward God's kingdom to come on earth as it is in heaven in pursuit of the vertical, horizontal, and cosmic redemptive vision for which Jesus died and rose again.[6]

There is a great temptation for us to use secular models to solve spiritual problems. This isn't to say that we can't glean insights from history and data and culture. After all, this entire world is God's world, and all truth is God's truth. We can declare with Abraham Kuyper, "There is not a square inch in the whole domain of our human existence over which Christ, who is Sovereign over all, does not cry, Mine!"[7] And yet we should be wary of allowing secular models, many of which deny biblical truth, to shape the way we see race or any other topic.

The first way many well-meaning Christians are tempted to use unbiblical frameworks when it comes to racial tensions is what is often called "colorblindness."[8] Typically when we think of ourselves as colorblind, we say things like, "When I see people, I don't see their color." In one sense, this is good. After all, Galatians 3:28 declares that when it comes to our salvation, there is "neither Jew nor Gentile, neither slave nor free." There is only one race, the human race and the new people of God saved by Christ. It's also good for us to be colorblind when it comes to the application of the law or in things like hiring preferences or access to opportunity in society. This was Martin Luther King Jr.'s dream, that one day his children would live in a country that would judge them not by color but by the content of their character.

But while we want our laws to be colorblind to ensure fairness and not discriminate based on race or ethnicity, and while we want to work for a society that allows equal opportunity regardless of color, and while we should not condition our hiring practices on color, colorblindness has a lot of problems.

Why is it not biblical to say, "I don't see color"? Because Scripture sees ethnicity not as a problem to be avoided but as a blessing to be acknowledged. God delights in the ethnic diversity of his creation, which forms a rich and full mosaic of the image of God. This is why Jesus, standing on the mountain and issuing commands to his disciples, urged them to take the gospel to "all nations" (Matt. 28:19), or as the Greek intends to say, "all *ethne*." The gospel doesn't wipe out our unique and beautiful ethnic heritage. The gospel redeems our ethnicity, and at the end of the age, we will see not a boring, unicolor, amorphous crowd standing before the throne of our risen king but people from "every nation, tribe, people and language" (Rev. 7:9).

It might be well-intended to say "I don't see your

color," but that says to someone, "I don't see the beautiful way God made you." My friend Trillia Newbell says it best: "I'm an African-American woman. I cannot—and crucially, I have no desire to—erase the fact that God made me this way. There's no hiding my milky-brown, freckled skin. I am who I am. When I walk into a room and I'm the only black woman, it's obvious. I know it; you know it; we all know it. It's ridiculous to pretend otherwise."[9]

It is ridiculous to pretend otherwise. I'm a white man, with a Jewish mother and a father of mixed European heritage. Not only should not I pretend not to see that but, like Trillia, I should rejoice in the way God formed me (Psalm 139). Colorblindness can also prevent us from seeing where race has played a factor in our history or has hurt minorities. For instance, it's hard for some to think through concepts like systemic racism. To be sure, many have wrongly used this idea to try to explain every kind of social disparity, falsely labeling every single institution as systemically racist. But as people of the Word, we do understand that while sin is personal and individual (Rom. 3:23) and every person is accountable to God (Rom. 14:12), it also has marbled its way through every facet of human life. Ephesians 6:12 reminds us that evil is corporate (principalities and powers). The prophets often spoke of God's judgment against whole nations for their sins. Governments, businesses, and institutions are run by and filled with sinners. And policies can be disproportionately aligned against a certain people group.

As a Jewish Christian, I'm keenly aware that a system

was devised in Germany to extinguish an entire people. While individual Nazis were responsible for atrocities committed against Jewish people, the system itself was demonic: designed to capture, imprison, and kill an entire race. Our American history of chattel slavery and Jim Crow laws is another example of systemic racism. A modern analog would be legalized abortion, which disproportionally kills black children.[10]

An equally wrong approach to racial issues is what some refer to as "antiracism," which is sometimes lumped under the umbrella of critical race theory (CRT). CRT is a legal and philosophical worldview. The aims of those who subscribe to its ideas also are well-meaning. We should all be "antiracist" if that means being against ethnic hatred and prejudice. But much of this philosophy, which I can't fully get into in a short chapter in this book, is not only unhelpful but unbiblical. The most popular proponents are folks like Ibram Kendi, author of *How to Be an Antiracist*, and Robin DiAngelo, author of *White Fragility*. Those books soared in popularity, even among evangelicals, in the wake of the murder of George Floyd by a Minneapolis police officer. This paradigm separates the world into two categories: oppressed and oppressor. Scholar Bruce Ashford outlines some of the problems with this worldview:

> Although CRT was founded as a theory about ethnic heritage in relation to power dynamics, it has come to function as an ideology—a comprehensive system of

thought wrapped around an idol. The idol embedded in CRT is not equality but equity—the achievement of equal outcomes for all our society's member groups. To the extent that equity is achieved, CRT proponents argue, society will be liberated from injustice.

Like all ideologies, CRT espouses a narrative that competes with the Bible's story of the world. Indeed, CRT offers a form of anti-religion as an alternative to Christian orthodoxy. Instead of a worldview that begins with all things created by God, CRT tends to begin its narrative about the world with human oppression. Rather than emphasizing that the truest thing about human persons is their relation to and accountability before God, CRT claims that the truest thing about human beings is that they are embedded in human groupings that form their identity.[11]

These teachings take true realities such as systemic sin and make that the entire narrative of human existence, as if the only thing about us are the identities that control our behaviors. It communicates that the only story about the world is a story of oppression. This is not only an impoverished way of seeing the world, as opposed to the way the Bible describes humanity, but it leads to unintended outcomes. George Yancey, a sociologist at Baylor and author of *Beyond Racial Division*, writes a critique of these antiracism models: "Anti-racism cannot provide us with complete solutions to the problem of racial alienation. It generates efforts to help deal with racial injustice, but the way it does so does not consider how these efforts create their own types of unfairness."[12]

Instead, Yancey encourages a better, more biblical model that he calls "mutual accountability" and "active listening." He urges Christians from all walks of life to take responsibility and to listen to those who are different from them in a way that offers give and take, push and pull, a willingness to hear what others are saying. "Both color-blindness and anti-racism are secular ideologies in that they are based on the notion that we can rely on human rationality to solve racial problems."[13] This is similar to what Tony Evans, longtime radio and television pastor, says in his important book *Kingdom Race Theology*:

Every Christian who names the name of Jesus Christ must be actively and purposefully involved in racial reconciliation, according to the Scriptures. Not division. Not blame. Not divisive speech. Not dismissiveness. Why? Because unity is what glorifies God and allows His presence to be visibly seen in and through His people. Like a football team, we may come from different backgrounds and ethnicities, but we are to be one team, wearing one uniform. There are different cultures and different backgrounds, but there is only one uniform. We are to head toward the same goal line together, which is the exaltation of Jesus Christ through His reconciled body, advancing God's kingdom agenda on earth through the individual, family, church, and community.[14]

If we care deeply about racial unity, we need to reject both of these extremes. We need to develop empathy for those who have experiences different from ours, to sit at tables with brothers and sisters who don't look like us, to resist the pundits and politicians who want to keep us divided. We need to be realistic about America's original sin of racism and its continually lingering effects, and we need to be realistic about the solutions, knowing that even as we work for a society that lives up to the idea of all men being created equal, we'll never fully achieve that utopia in a fallen world. We won't fully solve the problem of race in the culture and even in the church in one generation, or perhaps even in a hundred generations. Wherever sinners gather, even redeemed sinners, there will always be the temptation to think of ourselves more highly than we ought (Rom. 12:3). What we can do, as members of Christ's body, is to ask ourselves how we can better love those who look different from us, who have different experiences and share different opinions.

Moving Forward: Lament, Humility, Grace, Hope

Racial divisions in our country seem so intractable today, so it's understandable that many are weary of even talking about it. I get that. But for the sake of the witness of the gospel, let's commit ourselves at least to pursuing unity where we can. Let's commit to displays of multiethnic unity where possible, knowing that in every context and given the weight of history, it's not always possible every Sunday in every location. Let's turn down the rhetoric and namecalling and tribalism among the people of God, especially in our own little circles of influence and in our churches and small groups.

This effort requires, I believe, four biblical traits. First, we should take the time and space to lament. It's right and proper for us to sit and lament both the way our culture is divided racially and the gross injustices in our nation's history. I dearly love this country and feel enormous pride every Fourth of July. I love reading about our great leaders and visiting our important monuments. Yet patriotism requires me to acknowledge our wrongs. I lament that for much of our history, we considered nonwhite races of God's image bearers to be less than human. The Bible devotes a lot of space to lament, especially of the prophets who wept over the sinful state of their country, and of Jesus, who wept over Jerusalem. So too can we. Isaac Adams, a black pastor in Alabama, writes this: "Before we rush to hope, let's make sure we sit in the sadness. Our God will sit there with us. He is near to the brokenhearted. And so we grieve freely. We lament deeply."[15]

We must also practice humility. We don't know everything there is to know about everything. We are tempted to assume the best about our motives and assume the worst about others'. We look in the mirror and see a hero and look at our brothers and sisters who might disagree as villains. Adams says, "Humility requires boldness because it exposes us to risk as we lower ourselves and put others' needs before our own. Being humble in these conversations means we admit that we may be wrong or that we may have messed up. It means we stop showing up at the table as if we have everything to say and nothing to learn."[16]

Humility requires us to examine our hearts and ask the Lord to expose sinful attitudes and patterns. It requires us to seek out brothers and sisters who disagree with us, whose experiences are different from ours. Lord, make us humble. I have a pastor friend who sees some of these things differently. Our friendship began, ironically, in disagreement. But the more I talked with him, the more I realized he had things to say that I needed to hear, good points he made that helped me see in a way I hadn't seen before.

A humble willingness to listen, by people on all sides, leads to grace. Grace for those who might not have the right words when talking about race. Grace for those who you think are not as enlightened as you or who you think have not studied the issues as well as you. We also need some grace for those who've gone before us. While we shouldn't whitewash history and treat our heroes as if they are unblemished, perhaps we might also recognize our own frailties when evaluating men and women from history.

It's easy to argue with a caricature, especially if we envision ourselves as heroes. But not everyone who cares deeply about racial reconciliation and laments racial disparities is a proponent of CRT who denies Scripture. In the same way, not everyone who has deep concerns about some secular proposals for racial problems is a white supremacist. Most people are trying to fumble their way through these issues.

Shai Linne, a pastor and musician in Philadelphia, writes:

> Bearing with one another in love means avoiding resentment and bitterness toward our brothers and sisters in Christ with whom we disagree. It's resisting the impulse to retaliate or punish those who have hurt us. In the ethnicity discussion, it means moving toward, rather than away from, fellow church members who just don't seem to get it when it comes to ethnicity. Bearing with one another in love means not automatically "cancelling" a Christian who says something foolish, unhelpful, or even sinful regarding ethnicity. Bearing with one another in love means having open arms, ready to extend forgiveness when a believer says something insensitive or hurtful regarding ethnicity. Bearing with one another in love means pressing through the layers of misunderstanding, trusting that God is at work to sanctify both you and the Christian you disagree with.[17]

We also, last, need hope. It's easy to be so cynical about race and the number of officer-involved shootings, a rise in crime, protests, calls to "cancel" someone, and division in the church. These things give us a lot of fodder for our discontent. Yet we should not give up on the opportunity for racial reconciliation, for ethnic unity, even in small ways, at small tables, with a few people who love Jesus. I'm weary, but I'm committed to staying at the table. I hope you are too. After all, we know that this work is work Jesus is going to finish. One day we will be present with our brothers and sisters from every nation, tribe, and tongue around the throne of our risen, victorious king. I'll leave you with a final word of hope from Shai Linne: "In Jesus' prayer in John 17:21–22, He prayed that the church would be one. . . . The Father always answers Jesus' prayers. Because of that, we can be assured that the unity of the church will be accomplished. It was purchased at the cross. We seek to walk in it now, knowing that it will be perfected in eternity."[18]

Recommended Reading

You'll notice I quote from a few more books than usual in this chapter. I did that intentionally. If you are interested in the work of racial reconciliation, I highly recommend these good books by faithful, godly, Bible-saturated brothers and sisters:

Beyond Racial Division by George Yancey
How to Heal Our Racial Divide by Derwin Gray
Kingdom Race Theology by Tony Evans
The New Reformation by Shai Linne
Redemptive Kingdom Diversity by Jarvis Williams
Talking about Race by Isaac Adams
United by Trillia Newbell

Chapter 9

The Worst Hurt

*I am deeply motivated to know God. I want
to know Him as He truly is, not through
the distorted reflection of those who called
themselves by His name. And I want to
make Him known to others as accurately,
winsomely, clearly, and compellingly as I can.*

—Anne Graham Lotz

I'm writing this late at night, a few days after a reconciliation meeting with a church member. We shook hands. We hugged. We're moving forward. But the hurt, like other church hurts, runs deep. Church people sometimes hurt people.

As I've written in previous chapters, I've experienced the best and worst of the church. This chapter is about the worst. We have to be honest with ourselves and admit that sometimes the most painful, difficult blows we face are delivered by fellow Christians.

It hurts to be hurt, but it hurts doubly to be hurt by people who claim the name of Jesus. We expect lost souls to act like lost souls, but when the knife is wielded by a fellow Christian, the pain hurts more and the wound goes deeper. Yet that's the reality of life as a follower of Jesus. Anne Graham Lotz, the daughter of evangelist Billy Graham, saw this up close. She wrote an entire book, *Wounded by God's People*, chronicling her own betrayals at the hands of fellow Christians and says this: "As I look back on my life, it saddens me to acknowledge that some of my most painful wounds were inflicted by religious people—God's people."[1]

Even Jesus was betrayed by someone close to him, one who had preached the gospel and whom God used to bring healing and salvation. It was Judas, who had earlier left everything to follow Jesus, who everyone assumed was a loyalist, who sold Jesus out for a half a year's wages.

Consider Paul's lament to the Philippians, a word written from prison, where he was serving time because of his refusal to stop preaching Christ: "The former preach Christ out of selfish ambition, not sincerely, supposing that they can stir up trouble for me while I am in chains" (Phil. 1:17).

Think about that. Paul is being persecuted for his faith and yet there are Christians who are trying to stir up trouble for him for personal gain. In his last letter, written to his protege Timothy as his execution by Rome drew closer, Paul laments a lack of support from fellow believers: "At my first defense, no one came to my support, but everyone deserted me. May it not be held against them. But the Lord stood at my side and gave me strength, so that through me the message might be fully proclaimed and all the Gentiles might hear it. And I was delivered from the lion's mouth. The Lord will rescue me from every evil attack and will bring me safely to his heavenly kingdom. To him be glory for ever and ever. Amen" (2 Tim. 4:16–18).

Imagine the hurt. Paul stood *alone* at his trial on the charge of preaching the gospel. We can imagine the way fellow Christians disappointed him. Some, likely, thought he was perhaps a bit too confrontational, that perhaps he could have softened the edges of the gospel so as not to arouse suspicion by the religious and civil authorities. Some, likely, assumed they'd articulate the gospel better and, had they been in Paul's sandals, might have made better arguments. And it's all too likely there were the first-century version of the online warriors we see today, finding reason to think Paul wasn't courageous enough or was too kind or deferential to his accusers. They, from the safety of their position, looked in the mirror and probably saw someone braver than the shipwrecked, beaten, and imprisoned apostle Paul.

I've experienced two life-shattering betrayals at the hands of God's people, and a thousand tiny cuts along the way. I wrote about one of these experiences in chapter 3, a moment that caused great pain early in my ministry. This was not over significant doctrinal issues or character issues but out of a sense of control. It was painful and I felt completely alone. The church where I was raised and spent thirty years of my life turned her back on me in a very public way because I chose a different model of ministry. Every person I knew there, every friend with whom I'd worked, shared lunch with, and even vacationed, either spoke against me or refused to defend me. Only a handful were even willing to hear me out.

As I wrote earlier, God was able to do a sweet work of forgiveness in me and I've since experienced peace and love for them. I've moved on in my life and God has used this experience to enrich and strengthen me, to teach me things about myself and about him I otherwise never would have learned.

More recently I faced another betrayal by a close friend, a conflict that spilled out into public and was a major news story for about two weeks. I was publicly fired for writing in favor of the COVID-19 vaccine. It was a period when I wondered whether I'd ever work again. God took great care of me in the wake of that surprising hurt and brought an overflow of friends to come alongside and care for us. God even used this experience to bring me further into my calling. I've since forgiven that hurt and have worked toward reconciliation. I'm at peace with the situation.

Yet these and other hurts run deep, don't they? The deep cuts caused me, at times, to doubt the goodness of God, to be cynical about the church, to find it hard to trust again. I don't know where you are as you read this chapter. Perhaps you've had a bad experience in church or have been seriously wounded by a fellow believer. I want this chapter to be an encouragement to you. I want you to know you are not alone and that God has a plan for you, even in your pain.

I also want to be clear that this chapter about church hurt is not about criminal acts such as sexual and physical abuse. Those who abuse in God's name should not be protected by Christian institutions and instead should be held accountable by the civil authorities. And their victims should be cared for in the best possible way.

Why Church People Hurt People

Why do church people hurt people? It seems so counterintuitive, doesn't it? If we are the people who represent Jesus to the world, how is it that Christians can often offend and wound so deeply?

It's especially difficult when people we've admired disappoint us this way. I can think of a pastor I grew up with who was influential in my life, and who matched me up with my future wife. The last years of his life were spent trying to hurt me. I've since forgiven him, but I remember wondering during that painful season how someone who had had such an impact on the kingdom of God could be so petty and vindictive.

I'm also thinking about a Christian author and speaker whose words were instrumental in my theological development who has now denied the faith. When he announced his "deconversion," I wept. I still wonder how someone whose ministry was so effective and life changing could abandon the faith. He didn't directly hurt me, of course, but I'm hurt because I care for his soul.

I'm thinking of a group of elders in a church once pastored by a dear friend. My friend did nothing but carefully shepherd the people, preach the Word, and seek to reach the community with the gospel. He was rewarded for his work with a coup, led by the staff, and found himself without his church and without a job. Today he's serving in a different kind of ministry, but still working through issues of trust and forgiveness.

I think of the shy teen who never felt accepted by her peers in the youth group. I think of the pastor's kids who saw their father treated horribly by his church. I think of event staff who have witnessed ugly, behind-the-scenes behavior by prominent Christians.

I've often struggled with this reality. But then I must

also recognize that I've hurt others deeply as well, often without even recognizing it. When I pastored my church, I'd hear from folks who'd left quietly because of something I said in the pulpit or perhaps offhand in the lobby. I tried my best to be a good shepherd of God's people, but I know that decisions I made, things I said that I shouldn't have said, could have wounded folks, often unintentionally.

I've had to go back to people, Christian brothers and sisters, to ask for their forgiveness. You have likely had to do this as well. The reality is that the church, God's people, is made up not of perfect people but of people in the process of becoming more like Jesus. And the journey of sanctification is a long and halting one.

The apostle John, once called a Son of Thunder for his violent temper, who later became known as the "apostle of love," reminds us that even though Christians are saved by Jesus and given new life, the process of change is slow and lifelong. "Dear friends, now we are children of God, and what we will be has not yet been made known. But we know that when Christ appears, we shall be like him, for we shall see him as he is" (1 John 3:2).

John, writing at the end of his life, after seeing the long slow work of sanctification in his own life and as a leader in the church, is essentially acknowledging that sin has so woven its way into the human experience that even the most committed, spiritual followers of Jesus have a long way to go to perfection. So long that "what we will be has not yet been made known."

I've been walking with Jesus for more than four decades.

I've gone to church almost every Sunday of my life. I've read my Bible cover to cover so many times. I'm seminary trained. I've even parsed a few Greek words. Yet there are some days I look at the ugliness of my heart and grow discouraged. The Spirit has a lot of work to do in me.

And he has a way to go in you and in all of our fellow brothers and sisters. The people in the pews every Sunday are a work, a long, slow, painful work in progress. The church is made up of sinners, redeemed sinners, but sinners nonetheless. We are changed by Christ but still capable of hurting each other, sometimes deeply, sometimes cruelly, sometimes intentionally.

I'm not trying to minimize in any way the betrayals I've suffered or the things done to you by Christians. I don't think the Scriptures ask us to do that. When Paul talks about the trials he has suffered at the hands of those whom he once considered friends, when Jesus predicts his disciples will abandon him on the night of his crucifixion, when David writes of his painful betrayals, they are expressing valid, human emotions. And so should we.

Yet we must recognize that church people hurt people because church people are, well, sinners. This is the story of Christianity, that sinners are the only people God has to work with. You don't have to look closely in Scripture to see our heroes' ugly flaws. I love what Stephen Mansfield says in his book *Healing Your Church Hurt*: "You must not think of them [the Hebrews 12 cloud of witnesses] as perfect saints who never suffered as we do. Instead, you must see them as the flawed and the betrayed and the wounded who simply chose to live above the programming of their pain."[2]

Broken Reflections of the Divine

When I think back, so many years ago, to that moment in my office when I was feeling the betrayal of the church I grew up in, how people who loved and cared for me could hurt me so deeply, I remember a praise song, "Come to Jesus," playing through my speakers. I recognized in that moment that in order to keep my faith, I had to separate the sinful actions of Jesus' followers from Jesus himself. This we have to do not just in the big moments of disappointment but in our daily interactions with our fellow brothers and sisters, and they also have to do it when we commit sins against them.

This is the point of the apostle John's word in 1 John as he reminds the church that while we are "sons of God" being transformed by Jesus, we still sin against each other: "If we claim to be without sin, we deceive ourselves and the truth is not in us. If we confess our sins, he is faithful and just and will forgive us our sins and purify us from all unrighteousness. If we claim we have not sinned, we make him out to be a liar and his word is not in us" (1 John 1:8–10).

This word was written to the church, reminding us of our heavenly inheritance and our earthly brokenness. Until we reach the shores of heaven, until Jesus returns for his bride, the church will always be made up of sinners, always be a bit broken, sometimes more, sometimes less.

Pastor Matt Chandler says that the brokenness of God's people shouldn't keep us from Jesus:

> I want to acknowledge church hurt. Betrayal is a real thing. . . . The disciples don't bail on Jesus because of Judas. They've got their eyes on Jesus. They're blown away by Jesus. They're not looking around going, "Oh, man, all these people were following him. And man, look at that. They're inconsistent." You're inconsistent. I'm inconsistent. This is the only community there is that celebrates the fact that we're all in process. Nobody is there yet. To demand that you get grace and nobody else does is self-righteousness. To punt on Jesus because some Christian you know isn't up to your standards is a dangerous place to stand before a living God.
>
> The church has always been a mess.[3]

Anne Graham Lotz writes this of the need to separate the sins of God's people from God himself: "Don't blame God for the behavior of the people who have wounded you. I understand the desperate desire to run from them, but not from Him."[4] I've wanted to run. I understand the impulse to run, but in those moments of pain, I recognized that it wasn't God hurting me but broken people who believe in God.

Let's meditate on the unjust sufferings of Christ. The cross reminds us that we have somewhere to bring our pain, even pain inflicted by God's people. Nobody understands rejection by your own people like Jesus does. Jesus came to "his own, and his own received him not" (John 1:11 KJV). He was nailed to a cross by hands he formed, and mocked by those whom he gave breath. He was abandoned by his closest friends, was denied by his even closer friends, and was betrayed by the one he trusted. If Jesus could sweat drops of blood in the garden while accepting the Father's will to bear the weight of my offenses against him, then I can endure the afflictions put upon me.

I've been disappointed, maligned, slandered by people who claim the name of Christ, and yet when I look up at Calvary's cross, I can't compare my hurts to the ones inflicted on the Son of God, who knew no sin. How can I say anything but what Paul said about himself? I am the worst of sinners (1 Tim. 1:15). Yes, I've been sinned against, but I also have sinned against others. If the wounded, beaten, barely breathing Jesus can say, "Father, forgive them," I can forgive those who've hurt me. What's more, I can look beyond my church hurt and see the one who defeated sin and death and the grave. And despite what has been done to me, it doesn't make Jesus' triumphant resurrection from death any less true. My church hurt doesn't make that tomb in the Middle East less empty.

Christianity, you see, is the one religion that doesn't deny the sins of its followers. The Bible isn't telling the story of a good people who deserved praise, but of a fallen people who were pursued by a loving God. Not only can we acknowledge the messiness of the church and the sins of fellow Christians, but we can also say that this is the unique part of our Christian story. God is redeeming and welcoming sinners. What's more, God is making all things new. The messiness, even of Christians, will one day be made whole and right. One day we will no longer be disappointed by fellow Christians and will no longer disappoint fellow Christians.

The Church Hurt Me and the Church Healed Me

While my deepest wounds have often come at the hands of the church, I have to admit that my deepest healing and hope have also come from the church. When I was ostracized by the church of my youth, it was faithful pastors and Christians who came alongside me, defended me, and helped me see Jesus. When I was fired from my job by a close friend in a public way, it was an outpouring of evangelical Christians who came alongside me and donated money and time that helped our family work its way through this difficult season. When Christians have hurt me, it has been Christians who have helped me.

A couple of years ago, a popular podcast by Christianity Today took an honest look at the implosion of a once-influential church. I listened to every episode of *The Rise and Fall of Mars Hill*. It was painful to see how a church and leaders who began with the desire to reach their community with the gospel fell to authoritarianism, corruption, and scandal. And yet I was struck by something journalist Ted Olsen said toward the end. Olsen has seen, up close, some of the worst scandals in the Christian church. It's part of his day job. And yet Olsen says his faith in the church is restored when he looks around at his own congregation and sees ordinary Christians doing their best to follow Jesus.[5] I feel this way too, that as much as we are prone to being disappointed by the church, we should also look around and see the work God is doing in the world through flawed but faithful people. Christians can hurt, but Christians can heal.

I know it's hard to imagine, if you are in the pit of despair, staring up at your pain, that you can trust the church again. But I want to tell you that Jesus is there with you in your disappointment and disillusionment. Perhaps you need to change churches, perhaps you can find reconciliation, but I want to urge you not to give up on the church.

So how do we process our church hurt and yet participate in the community of faith? Here are some things that have helped me and that I hope will help you:

1. We should ask others whether they are seeing what we are seeing. This is one way to make sure the offenses are real and not imagined. There have been times when I felt like another believer was intentionally working against me, but once I got the whole story, I realized that it was my misperception of his motives and that his desire was not to hurt me. This isn't always what our hearts want to do, but it's important we separate our sometimes-skewed perception from reality. Therefore, it's

important to ask others whether they are seeing what we are seeing.

2. If we truly have been hurt by other believers' actions, we should not hesitate to acknowledge it. Wishing it away doesn't do us any good. And then we should ask ourselves whether this is merely an annoying offense that can be met with forbearance (Col. 3:12) or it's an offense serious enough to require confrontation (Matt. 18:15–20). If the conflict involves members of our church, we should do our best not to let it divide the community but should work with the leaders of the church. Sometimes conflict is so bad it might require us to find another Christian community. And yet sometimes conflict can be healthy, handled well by all parties, and lead to growth.

3. We should seek out wisdom from mature Christian brothers and sisters. The temptation amid betrayal or pain or hurt is to react in anger, but it is foolish to make decisions in the heat of the moment, when we are running on adrenaline and emotion. Being isolated and alone is a recipe for disaster. I have a policy of not making big decisions when I'm in this state.

4. We should work on the process of forgiveness and reconciliation, but this will take time. It is often uneven and difficult. For serious offenses against us, we might seek counseling or therapy from a trusted Christian counselor who can help us work through the layers of our pain.

5. We should recommit to the spiritual disciplines of prayer and Bible reading and meditation. Sometimes it can be hard to approach God when we've been hurt so deeply. But hearing the Lord's words is important in this moment. Crying out to God in pain and despair is important in this moment. Meditating on God's promises is important in this moment.

6. We should resist the urge to make our situation all-consuming. I struggle with this mightily and in the midst of crisis often neglect rest and nutrition and the needs of those around me. This is where good friends and the support of our families can help us stay grounded.

A Final Plea

> *Upon his authority [Jesus] gives the world*
> *the right to judge whether you and I are*
> *born-again Christians on the basis of our*
> *observable love toward all Christians.*

> **—Francis Schaeffer**, *The Mark of the Christian*

I want to end with a final, short plea. I've poured out my heart in these pages, and I pray that God will use these words to catalyze a movement toward faithful, biblical, orthodox gospel unity among his people.

My plea for unity is simple. I desire it because Jesus desires it and prayed for it (John 17). It's the will of the Father (Psalm 133). We should want what Jesus wants. His body is not divided, even though we act and live, too often, as if it is.

Our visible unity among differences in race and class and income level and political persuasion is a powerful testimony to the validity and truth of the gospel. As much as I can, as much as you can, as much as we all can, let's love our brothers and sisters, fight for the truth that has been handed down to us, and work together to tell the world about the good news of the gospel.

Disunity not only divides us but also distracts us from our mission. Billions of people walking this earth do not know Jesus. They deserve to hear about a God who sent his only Son, Jesus, who was fully God and fully man, to save them from their sin. They deserve to learn how they can find peace with God and be reunited with their creator. They deserve the comfort of knowing that the broken world in which they struggle will one day give way to a restored heaven and earth.

I am not one to talk much about spiritual warfare, perhaps because I've seen many people's tendency to falsely attribute everything bad to the spirit world. (Or maybe I'm still haunted by reading *This Present Darkness* in high school.) However, we should recognize that we have an enemy who seeks to thwart the work of God's church. I'm convinced there is much spiritual warfare behind our disunity, especially on tertiary issues. First Peter 5:8 reminds us that our enemy prowls around seeking whom he may devour. Part of his devouring work is to get Christians fighting so they will be powerless to share the gospel that frees lost souls from his grasp (2 Tim. 2:25–26).

We live in strange, interesting, and often perilous times. This is not a moment for the church to descend into carnal factions. It is a moment for a united witness against the darkness of the age. If you are concerned about cultural shifts, if you value freedom for Christian witness in the West, you should be driven not to division but to unity.

None of us can solve the problem of disunity at the big, national level, but we can each take steps in our circles of influence. We can do this by working hard to find common ground with Christians who are different from us. Paul says he so desires to build relationships with those who don't yet know the love of Jesus that he searches for common ground:

For when I preach the gospel, I cannot boast, since I am compelled to preach. Woe to me if I do not preach the gospel! If I preach voluntarily, I have a reward; if not voluntarily, I am simply discharging the trust committed to me. What then is my reward? Just this: that in preaching the gospel I may offer it free of charge, and so not make full use of my rights as a preacher of the gospel.

Though I am free and belong to no one, I have made myself a slave to everyone, to win as many as possible. To the Jews I became like a Jew, to win the Jews. To those under the law I became like one under the law (though I myself am not under the law), so as to win those under the law. To those not having the law I became like one not having the law (though I am not free from God's law but am under Christ's law), so as to win those not having the law. To the weak I became weak, to win the weak. I have become all things to all people, so that by all possible means I might save some. I do all this for the sake of the gospel, that I may share in its blessings.

—1 Corinthians 9:16–23

Paul is talking here about building relationships with unbelievers. And so should we be constantly looking for relational bridges to the unreached. Yet we must ask ourselves how much more we should be looking for relational bridges to our brothers and sisters in Christ.

Paul later says, "Therefore, as we have opportunity, let

us do good to all people, especially to those who belong to the family of believers" (Gal. 6:10).

I like Paul's realism here. "As much as possible." In a fallen world, friendship is not always possible. And yet when we have opportunity, we should do good, especially to those to whom we are spiritually related. As much as you can, wherever you can, as much as it depends on you, live at peace.

So maybe the close of this book is the start of something in your life and in mine—a relationship mended, a conflict resolved, a grudge lifted off our backs and given over to Jesus.

I pray my words have been helpful to you, your family, your church, or your organization as you endeavor to seek "the unity of the Spirit through the bond of peace" (Eph. 4:3).

May we be agents of grace.

Acknowledgments

Many folks helped to make this book possible. There's my middle-school teacher who sparked my future as a writer by commending some of my essays. There's my first boss, who urged me to seek publication for my work. There's the editor who took a chance on me with my first book project. There's my wonderful father and mother, who bequeathed to me the gospel and a love for the church, and who always told me, from an early age, that I could write.

This book has an especially important circle of heroes. I wrote it while moving from Tennessee to Texas, a time of upheaval. This meant my wife, Angela, performed superhuman feats in managing our move and in somehow carving out time for me to finish the book. I'm thankful to her for believing always in my work, for being a champion, for being a fellow joyful warrior for more than two decades of marriage. She is a true agent of grace in my life. My kids also deserve recognition for supporting their dad in the good times and the bad, and for their willingness to go where the Lord is calling. Grace, Daniel, Emma, Lily: I'm proud of all of you.

Acknowledgments

I'm writing on the campus of Southwestern Baptist Theological Seminary, where I serve as director of the Land Center for Faith and Culture. I'm grateful to our president, David Dockery, a man of uncommon servant leadership, and for my colleagues, who have taught me so much.

I also want to thank my amazing literary agent, Erik Wolgemuth, who has been a constant source of wisdom over the last few years, helping me make good decisions about my projects, tolerating my sudden phone calls and texts with new ideas for books, and helping to make this project happen. I'm thankful to Andy Rogers at Zondervan, who could see the vision for this, my most personal book to date. Thank you for your patient edits and suggestions that helped polish my words.

I also want to thank a few close friends who are such gifts. My friend and mentor, Daryl. My text-thread buddies: you know who you are. My friends Travis and DJ and Josh and Andrew and Joseph and Eddie and Michael and Jason and Marie and Lindsay and Brent. Thank you for being there for me.

Last, I want to thank the Lord for allowing me yet another opportunity to be a conduit of his love to those who are on the other end of my words.

Notes

Foreword

1. "Pastors' Views on How COVID-19 Is Affecting Their Church July 2020: Survey of American Protestant Pastors," LifeWay Research, accessed November 12, 2022, http://research.lifeway.com/wp-content/uploads/2020/07 /Coronavirus-Pastors-Full-Report-July-2020.pdf.

Chapter 1: What Does Love Require?

1. Rhonda Vincent, "You Don't Love God If You Don't Love Your Neighbor," https://www.youtube.com/watch?v =IR2rpVd5Lwo.
2. Earl S. Kalland, "398 קָבַד," in *Theological Wordbook of the Old Testament*, ed. R. Laird Harris, Gleason L. Archer Jr., and Bruce K. Waltke (Chicago: Moody, 1999), 177–78.
3. Chris L. Firestone and Alex H. Pierce, *Why Does Friendship Matter?* Questions for Restless Minds (Bellingham, WA: Lexham Press, 2021), 27–28.
4. Scott Sauls, *A Gentle Answer: Our "Secret Weapon" in an Age of Us against Them* (Nashville: Thomas Nelson, 2020), xxv.
5. Francis Schaeffer, *The Mark of a Christian*, in *The Complete Works of Francis A. Schaeffer*, vol. 4, *A Christian*

View of the Church, 2nd ed. (Wheaton, IL: Crossway, 1985), 198.

6. Erik Raymond, "Love Believes All Things," Gospel Coalition, August 26, 2015, www.thegospelcoalition.org /blogs/erik-raymond/love-believes-all-things/.

7. Firestone and Pierce, *Why Does Friendship Matter?* 64.

8. Schaeffer, *Mark of a Christian*, 191.

9. Megan Hill, "Three Ways God Loves the Church (and You Should Too)," Core Christianity, July 21, 2020, https:// corechristianity.com/resource-library/articles/3-ways -god-loves-the-church-and-you-should-too/.

10. Schaeffer, *Mark of a Christian*, 194.

Chapter 2: The Blood-Stained Banner

1. Timothy George and John Woodbridge, *The Mark of Jesus: Loving in a Way the World Can See* (Chicago: Moody, 2005), 35.

2. Gavin Ortlund, *Finding the Right Hills to Die On: The Case for Theological Triage* (Wheaton, IL: Crossway, 2020), 33.

3. Ortlund, *Finding the Right Hills*, 33.

4. George and Woodbridge, *Mark of Jesus*, 37.

5. Francis Chan, *Until Unity* (Colorado Springs: Cook, 2021), 28.

6. Chan, *Until Unity*, 19.

7. Chan, *Until Unity*, 42.

Chapter 3: Drinking Poison

1. Read the whole story in Matthew 18:21–35.

2. Corrie ten Boom, "Guideposts Classics: Corrie ten Boom on Forgiveness," *Guideposts*, accessed July 24, 2014, https://guideposts.org/positive-living/guideposts-classics -corrie-ten-boom-forgiveness/.

3. Mark Berman, "'I Forgive You.' Relatives of Charleston

Church Shooting Victims Address Dylann Roof," *Washington Post*, June 19, 2015, www.washingtonpost .com/news/post-nation/wp/2015/06/19/i-forgive-you -relatives-of-charleston-church-victims-address-dylann -roof/.

Chapter 4: Our Glorious Mess

1. Read the complete epic story in 1 Kings 18:16–46.
2. Jon Tyson (@JonTyson), "There is a fine line," Twitter, March 12, 2022, twitter.com/JonTyson/status /1502743230537994247.
3. "Sarah Eekhoff Zylstra," Gospel Coalition, accessed March 12, 2022, www.thegospelcoalition.org/profile /sarah-eekhoff-zylstra.
4. Sarah Eekhoff Zylstra, "How an Unlikely Church Is Reaching Refugees," Gospel Coalition, November 1, 2021, www.thegospelcoalition.org/article/church-refugees.
5. Sarah Eekhoff Zylstra, "The Growth of Christianity in the World's First Atheist Country," Gospel Coalition, January 18, 2022, www.thegospelcoalition.org/article /christianity-atheist-country.
6. Kelly Chibale and Sarah Eekhoff Zylstra, "God's Mercy in a New Malaria Vaccine," Gospel Coalition, November 5, 2021, www.thegospelcoalition.org/article/malaria-vaccine.
7. Collin Hansen and Sarah Eekhoff Zylstra, *Gospel Bound: Living with Resolute Hope in an Anxious Age* (Colorado Springs: Multnomah, 2021).
8. Megan Hill, *A Place to Belong: Learning to Love the Local Church* (Wheaton, IL: Crossway, 2020), 15–16.
9. Hill, *Place to Belong*, 97.
10. Dustin Benge, "Help! I Love Jesus but Not the Church," Crossway, March 10, 2022, www.crossway.org/articles /help-i-love-jesus-but-not-the-church/.

Chapter 5: Christian Famous

1. "Billy Graham Trivia: What Did Billy Graham Say about Getting a Star on the Hollywood Walk of Fame?" Billy Graham Evangelistic Association, July 27, 2017, https//billygraham.org/story/billy-graham-trivia-billy -grahams-hopes-upon-name-inscribed-hollywoods-walk -fame.

2. Christine Rosen, "'The Internet Is Not What You Think It Is' Review: Warning! This Site Isn't Safe," *Wall Street Journal*, March 14, 2022, www.wsj.com/articles /the-internet-is-not-what-you-think-it-is-review-warning -this-site-isnt-safe-11647296267.

3. Tim Chester, *Stott on the Christian Life* (Wheaton, IL: Crossway, 2020), 228.

4. Mark Leibovich, "The Man the White House Wakes Up To," *New York Times*, April 21, 2010, www.nytimes .com/2010/04/25/magazine/25allen-t.html.

5. Jim VandeHei, "What I've Learned from Mike Allen and Mister Rogers," *Axios*, March 18, 2022, www.axios.com /mike-allen-mister-rogers-leadership-modesty-052cfdf7 -4b75-4a9d-a07c-4c68ffde1cc1.html.

6. Mark Sayers, *A Non-Anxious Presence: How a Changing and Complex World Will Create a Remnant of Renewed Christian Leaders* (Chicago: Moody, 2022).

Chapter 6: The Good Fight

1. A good recap of this controversy can be found in Justin Taylor, "Rob Bell Revisited: Five Years Later," Gospel Coalition, June 2, 2016, www.thegospelcoalition.org /blogs/justin-taylor/rob-bell-revisited-5-years-later.

2. John Stott, *Evangelical Truth: A Personal Plea for Unity, Integrity and Faithfulness*, Global Christian Library (2003; Carlisle, UK: Langham Global Library, 2013), 117.

3. John Piper, "TULIP: Introduction," Desiring God, March 7, 2008, www.desiringgod.org/messages/tulip -introduction-session-1.

4. R. Albert Mohler Jr., "A Call for Theological Triage and Christian Maturity," Albert Mohler, May 20, 2004, albertmohler.com/2004/05/20/a-call-for-theological -triage-and-christian-maturity-2.

5. Gavin Ortlund, *Finding the Right Hills to Die On: The Case for Theological Triage* (Wheaton, IL: Crossway, 2020), 47, italics in original.

6. Mohler, "Call for Theological Triage."

7. For a helpful explanation of first-tier doctrines, see Trevin Wax, *The Thrill of Orthodoxy: Rediscovering the Adventure of Christian Faith* (Downers Grove, IL: InterVarsity Press, 2022).

8. S. Donald Fortson III and Rollin G. Grams, *Unchanging Witness: The Consistent Christian Teaching on Homosexuality in Scripture and Tradition* (Nashville: B&H Academic, 2016), 27.

9. Steven D. Smith, *Pagans and Christians in the City: Culture Wars from the Tiber to the Potomac* (Grand Rapids: Eerdmans, 2018); Kyle Harper, *From Shame to Sin: The Christian Transformation of Sexual Morality in Late Antiquity*, reprint (Cambridge, MA: Harvard Univ. Press, 2016).

10. To explore this further, check out chapter 9 of Daniel Darling, *The Dignity Revolution: Reclaiming God's Rich Vision for Humanity* (Epsom, UK: Good Book Company, 2018).

Chapter 7: Religion and Politics

1. C. S. Lewis, *The Great Divorce*, rev. ed. (San Francisco: HarperOne, 2015), 96.

2. Scott Sauls, *A Gentle Answer: Our "Secret Weapon" in an Age of Us against Them* (Nashville: Thomas Nelson, 2020), xix.

3. Cal Thomas, "Beckel and Me: An Odd Couple," *News Herald*, March 6, 2022, www.news-herald.com/2022 /03/06/beckel-and-me-an-odd-couple-ca-thomas.

4. David French, "Getting 'More Christians into Politics' Is the Wrong Christian Goal," *Dispatch*, May 27, 2022, https://frenchpress.thedispatch.com/p/getting-more -christians-into-politics.

5. Michael Wear (@MichaelRWear), "Christians: The crisis is not that you are politically homeless," Twitter, March 28, 2017, https://twitter.com/MichaelRWear /status/846912054162264064.

Chapter 8: Nation, Tribe, Tongue

1. Trevor Atwood, *The Church and the Racial Divide: Finding Unity in the Race-Transcending Gospel*, ed. Daniel Darling and Trillia Newbell (Nashville: LifeWay Press, 2019); Daniel Darling, "Known, Seen, and Designed by God," in *Ministers of Reconciliation: Preaching on Race and the Gospel*, ed. Daniel Darling (Bellingham, WA: Lexham Press, 2021).

2. "Resolution on Racial Reconciliation on the 150th Anniversary of the Southern Baptist Convention," SBC, June 1, 1995, www.sbc.net/resource-library/resolutions /resolution-on-racial-reconciliation-on-the-150th -anniversary-of-the-southern-baptist-convention/.

3. Ronnie Floyd, "A Statistical Analysis of Growth in SBC Congregations by Race and Ethnicity from 1990–2018," *Arkansas Baptist News*, December 11, 2020, https:// arkansasbaptist.org/post/a-statistical-analysis-of-growth-in -sbc-congregations-by-race-and-ethnicity-from-1990-2018/.

4. Derwin L. Gray, *How to Heal Our Racial Divide: What*

the Bible Says, and the First Christians Knew, about Racial
Reconciliation (Carol Stream, IL: Tyndale Momentum,
2022), 9, 28.

5. Gray, How to Heal Our Racial Divide, 29.

6. Jarvis J. Williams, Redemptive Kingdom Diversity: A
Biblical Theology of the People of God (Grand Rapids: Baker
Academic, 2021), 173.

7. Abraham Kuyper, Abraham Kuyper: A Centennial Reader
(Grand Rapids: Eerdmans, 1998), 461.

8. I am indebted to George Yancey's excellent work for
the framework of colorblindness and antiracism as well-
meaning but misguided approaches to racial tension.
George A. Yancey, Beyond Racial Division: A Unifying
Alternative to Colorblindness and Antiracism (Downers
Grove, IL: InterVarsity Press, 2022).

9. Trillia Newbell, "Four Reasons You Shouldn't Be
Colorblind," Gospel Coalition, August 24, 2017, www
.thegospelcoalition.org/article/4-reasons-you-shouldnt
-be-colorblind.

10. Carole Novielli, "Abortions Reach Highest Percentage
among Black Women since 2000," Live Action,
December 11, 2019, www.liveaction.org/news/abortions
-highest-percentage-black-women-2000.

11. Bruce Ashford, "Critical Race Theory: Plundering the
Egyptians or Worshiping Ba'al?" Public Discourse, June 6,
2021, www.thepublicdiscourse.com/2021/06/76185.

12. Yancey, Beyond Racial Division, 98.

13. Yancey, Beyond Racial Division, 135.

14. Tony Evans, Kingdom Race Theology: God's Answer to Our
Racial Crisis (Chicago: Moody, 2022), 64.

15. Isaac Adams, Talking about Race: Gospel Hope for Hard
Conversations (Grand Rapids: Zondervan Reflective,
2022), 108.

16. Adams, *Talking about Race*, 149.
17. Shai Linne, *The New Reformation: Finding Hope in the Fight for Ethnic Unity* (Chicago: Moody, 2021), 166.
18. Linne, *New Reformation*, 208.

Chapter 9: The Worst Hurt

1. Anne Graham Lotz, *Wounded by God's People: Discovering How God's Love Heals Our Hearts* (Grand Rapids: Zondervan, 2013).
2. Stephen Mansfield, *Healing Your Church Hurt: What to Do When You Still Love God but Have Been Wounded by His People* (Carol Stream, IL: Tyndale, 2012), 39.
3. The Village Church—Flower Mound, *A Gospel Call—Sermons—Matt Chandler—2/13/22*, YouTube, accessed November 11, 2022, www.youtube.com/watch?v=Ymi2EPH2VUk.
4. Graham Lotz, *Wounded by God's People*.
5. Mike Cosper, "Bonus Episode: I Kissed Christianity Goodbye," *The Rise and Fall of Mars Hill* (podcast), August 19, 2021, www.christianitytoday.com/ct/podcasts/rise-and-fall-of-mars-hill/joshua-harris-mars-hill-podcast-kissed-christianity-goodbye.html.